T0341497

CHARLOTTE BARLOW

COERCION AND WOMEN CO-OFFENDERS

A gendered pathway into crime

POLICY PRESS SHORTS RESEARCH

First published in Great Britain in 2016 by

Policy Press
University of Bristol
1-9 Old Park Hill
Bristol
BS2 8BB
UK
t: +44 (0)117 954 5940
pp-info@bristol.ac.uk
www.policypress.co.uk

North America office:
Policy Press
c/o The University of Chicago Press
1427 East 60th Street
Chicago, IL 60637, USA
t: +1 773 702 7700
f: +1 773 702 9756
sales@press.uchicago.edu
www.press.uchicago.edu

© Policy Press 2016

British Library Cataloguing in Publication Data
A catalogue record for this book is available from the British Library.

Library of Congress Cataloging-in-Publication Data
A catalog record for this book has been requested.

ISBN 978-1-4473-3098-1 (hardcover)
ISBN 978-1-4473-3100-1 (ePub)
ISBN 978-1-4473-3101-8 (Mobi)

The right of Charlotte Barlow to be identified as the author of this work has been asserted by her in accordance with the Copyright, Designs and Patents Act 1988.

All rights reserved: no part of this publication may be reproduced, stored in a retrieval system, or transmitted in any form or by any means, electronic, mechanical, photocopying, recording, or otherwise without the prior permission of Policy Press.

The statements and opinions contained within this publication are solely those of the author and not of the University of Bristol or Policy Press. The University of Bristol and Policy Press disclaim responsibility for any injury to persons or property resulting from any material published in this publication.

Policy Press works to counter discrimination on grounds of gender, race, disability, age and sexuality.

Cover design by Policy Press
Front cover: image kindly supplied by iStock
Printed and bound in Great Britain by CPI Group (UK) Ltd, Croydon, CR0 4YY
Policy Press uses environmentally responsible print partners

Contents

Acknowledgements

This book is dedicated to a number of important people, who have helped and supported me throughout the research and writing process. First, my partner, Johnny, who provides me with continual support and encouragement. Also, my Mum, Dad, Gemma, Matt, Elanor-Mai and Annie Rose – my wonderful family who constantly experience the high and lows of my research.

A special mention also goes to my fantastic PhD supervisors, Professor Sandra Walklate and Professor Karen Ross. Both are wonderful, inspiring women and I will be forever grateful for the opportunities and support that they have given to me.

INTRODUCTION

There is a growing body of literature which supports the claim that women follow distinct and often gendered pathways into crime (Daly, 1994; Belknap and Holsinger, 2006), some of which are defined by their co-offending with a male partner. Coercion has been increasingly acknowledged as a pathway into crime for some female offenders, particularly those whose relationship with their male partner/co-offender is characterised by violence, abuse, control and/or obsession (Barlow, 2014; Jones, 2008; Richie, 1996; Welle and Falkin, 2000). This research uses a case study approach of four women co-accused with a man with whom they are in an intimate (real or imagined) relationship. Each of the women also utilised coercion as part of their defence during their trial, albeit to differing extents, and this research considers the legal and media representation of each of the cases. These women are high-profile examples of co-accused, potentially coerced women, whose cases have occurred within the last 15 years, thus providing a broad overview of the phenomenon. Having been granted access to the women's case and court file documents, I am able to explore the legal and media representation of the women. This allows a critical discussion of the ways in which the media represented the trials, thus enabling a comprehensive understanding of the social construction of coerced women more broadly.

In doing so, this book is divided into six chapters. Chapter one discusses existing literature and explores the dominant ways in which female offenders and co-offenders are represented in media and legal discourse, particularly considering motifs such as 'mad or bad'. Chapter Two introduces the concept of coercion as a pathway into crime and explores a range of literature and perspectives related to this topic. The feminist methodological approach utilised in this research is outlined in Chapter Three and the benefits of using a case study approach and a combination of comparative documents as data sources, such as newspapers and case file material, is also discussed. Chapter Four discusses the media and legal representation of the co-offending women case-studies, particularly considering motifs such as 'bad mother', 'mythical monster' and 'other', as well as exploring the construction of the women's defence and perspectives. The alternative conceptual framework of a 'continuum of coercion' is discussed in Chapter Five, which outlines the ways in which abusive, controlling and/or obsessive relationships with a male partner/co-offender may influence a woman's 'decision' to offend. The final chapter (Chapter Six) considers the ways in which this feminist, critical understanding of coercion may lead to a more nuanced understanding of co-offending women's pathways into crime, while emphasising the importance of understanding agency and 'choice' within the context of such relationships.

ONE
MEDIATED REPRESENTATIONS AND UNDERSTANDINGS OF CO-OFFENDING WOMEN

Introduction

This chapter outlines the existing literature which explores the dominant ways in which female offenders and co-offenders are represented in media, legal discourse and criminology more broadly. It also considers the ways in which gendered constructions, such as 'bad mother' (Barnett, 2006), 'evil manipulator' (Jewkes, 2015) and 'mythical monster' (Heidensohn, 1996; Jewkes, 2015) permeate media representations of female offenders/co-offenders. The chapter highlights the ways in which gender role expectations and patriarchal values infiltrate the social construction and criminological understandings of female offenders.

The dichotomies of 'man' and 'woman' and malestream criminology

The categories of 'man' and 'woman' are viewed as being in opposition to each other within academic disciplines, such as criminology, the natural sciences, psychology and sociology, but this is also applicable to western societies more broadly. For example, women have historically been defined by their nature, yet men continue to be defined as 'rational and cultured' beings (Sydie, 1987). This distinction has led to hierarchical social relations characterised by subordination and domination between men and women which, in turn, are seen to be natural, inevitable and unchangeable (Sydie, 1987). Such historical sex segregation has led to the pervasive view that women are inferior and defined by their 'natural' biology, whereas men are classified predominantly as reasonable and rational knowers (Russet, 1989; Sydie, 1987).

Such distinctions between the 'reasonable' man and the 'pathologically deficient' woman has led to the development of additional, pervasive dichotomies between the sexes. For example, it is often presumed and asserted that men are active beings and knowers, whereas women are subjective and passive (Sydie, 1987). Within the context of criminology, from the nineteenth century onwards, due to the birth of natural sciences, biology and Darwinism, positivism became the universal explanation of crime. This led to further biological based distinctions between women and men. According to Russet (1989), the most influential principle of 'sexual science' with regard to criminology during this period was biogenetics and its associated concept of atavism. Atavism 'described a situation in which an individual member of a species could be identified as a throwback to an earlier genetic period' (Walklate, 2001: 22). Lombroso and Ferrero were two of the lead thinkers within this area of thought and they argued that the criminal had a close biological relationship and resemblance to pre-historic savages.

Lombroso and Ferrero were predominantly concerned with understanding the male offender and even when the concept of the female offender was explored by such thinkers, she was categorised as an aberration from the 'normal' woman and thus a deviation against the feminine ideal (Evans and Jamieson, 2008). If we consider this alongside the physical anthropological belief that women were anatomically more childlike and infantile in comparison to men (Ellis, 1984), it gives a clear indication of how women were considered within criminology during this period in particular. Victorian science viewed women as a 'developmental anomaly' (Russet, 1989: 74). Lombroso and Ferrero (1895) believed that women's development was arrested at an earlier stage than men and that they subsequently did not have the same intellectual ability or power of reason.

The nineteenth century definitions and distinctions between the sexes still have significant influence today, particularly within criminological thinking. As highlighted by Walklate (2001: 24), Lombroso and Ferrero (1895) and other similar minded academics of the nineteenth century, have 'framed the way in which thinking about males and females and masculinity and femininity has been constructed', highlighting the reductionist nature of such deterministic, male dominated theories (Naffine, 1987; Harding, 1981). Consequently, certain assumptions, such as female passivity and the denial of agency and creativity for female offenders, continue to resonate in more contemporary accounts of female offending (Evans and Jamieson, 2008).

The same can be said for the late nineteenth-century criminological shift from physical anthropology to the psychology and personality of offenders. As highlighted by Russet (1989: 42), 'if men characteristically thought, women characteristically felt'. Within psychology during the Victorian period in particular, women were defined by their emotions and the perceived dangers of this emotional tendency, which centred around the belief that women were more likely to break away from reason and in extreme cases, the result was believed to be hysteria and unreasonable temper (Russet, 1989). Freud argued that women's emotional tendencies and frail temperament led them to be hysterical beings and psychologically weak in comparison to their male counterparts (Sydie, 1987). It has been suggested by various commentators (for example, Lloyd, 1995; Ballinger, 2000) that such pervasive beliefs about women's psychological inferiority led to particular treatment and perceptions of women who committed criminal offences. Such beliefs continue to resonate in more recent years, such as the suggested chivalry of men towards female offenders and the categorisation of the female offender as being 'mad' or 'bad' (discussed below). This dichotomisation is particularly applicable to the four women discussed here, as outlined in later analysis chapters.

Overall, such perspectives fail to acknowledge that gender is a social construct, rather than a biological characteristic, with masculinity and femininity being socially assessed based on the performance of gender (Butler, 1990; West and Zimmerman, 1987).

With this in mind, as argued by Bem (1993), contemporary society teaches people to understand gender through the lenses of androcentrism (male experience being the most significant), gender polarisation (treating masculinity and femininity as opposite poles of the same dimension) and biological essentialism (a deeply rooted belief that differences between the sexes are natural). Gender is a key determinant of likely involvement in offending behaviour, yet the importance of gender has not always been reflected in the development of criminological thought, as such knowledge has always been based on the assumption that crime is men's work and not women's (Evans and Jamieson, 2008; Walklate, 2001). The study of the 'criminal man' has dominated the development of criminological thought and thus 'criminal women' have mostly been excluded. The various deficiencies of malestream criminology previously discussed have been criticised by feminist thinkers, who have argued that a gendered perspective would make women more visible within criminology and would also 'dismantle or fracture the limitations of existing knowledges, boundaries and traditional methodologies' (Gelsthorpe, 2003: 8; Walklate, 2001; Heidensohn, 1996; Smart, 1976).

Overall, men and women have historically been defined by their biology within traditional criminological theories, but in differing ways. Women's offending has been persistently reduced to their inferior nature and biology, even within theories which have no biological focus, such as sub-cultural theories (Russet, 1989). Despite early criminological thinkers, such as Lombroso and Ferrero discussing the atavistic male criminal, male offenders have historically been defined by their ability to reason, their creative energy and their offending agency. The pervasive dichotomy of the 'nature' of women versus the 'reason' of men (Sydie, 1987) has defined traditional criminological thought and has subsequently led to the male offender to be viewed as the norm and the female offender described as the abnormal, 'other', as exemplified by the four co-accused women analysed here.

Women offenders as 'others'

Female offending is often individualised, pathologised and explained by over-simplistic and deterministic explanations such as being inherently evil, 'unhinged' or weak in legal and media discourse (Myers and Wight, 1996; Lavie-Dinur et al, 2013; Naylor, 2001; Barnett, 2006). This collectively leads to female offenders being viewed as 'others' or located as being a distinctly different type of person to the rest of society (Barlow, 2015b). 'Othering' is a process whereby certain individuals or groups are either directly or indirectly excluded from society, usually due to their being perceived as a threat to the social order (Riggins, 1997; Ajzenstandt and Shapira, 2012). Constructing individuals or groups as 'others' marks the normative boundaries of society, where the 'other' is mostly excluded serving to create distinct boundaries between 'us' and 'them' (Riggins, 1997; Young, 1999). Within the context of crime and deviance, it has been argued that 'othering' stems from societal ontological insecurity in late modernity, as creating 'others' is a direct response to a more diverse social order (Young, 1999).

Female offenders are constructed as the 'other' within the context of both the law and media, as both institutions are 'constructed around a masculine subject and an associated set of masculine characteristics' (Davies, 1997: 23; Ballinger, 2012; Carline, 2005; Naffine, 1996). Therefore, by their very nature, their experiences and perspectives are viewed to be outside the masculine norms associated with and perpetuated throughout such institutions. Journalists in particular often reinforce the 'otherness' of female offenders, particularly those who commit serious and/or violent offences, by regularly utilising demonising language to construct female offenders as the antithesis of good women (Jewkes, 2015). This is particularly the case for women who commit serious offences, such as crimes against children, as such women are guilty of breaking 'every culturally sanctioned code of femininity and womanhood' (Jewkes, 2015: 121). However, it is argued here that gendered discourse is applied to most, if not all, cases of female offending, regardless of the crime committed. Female offending, by its very nature, is viewed to be 'other', therefore such women are pathologised and 'othered' in an attempt to emphasise their 'difference' (Myers and Wight, 1996).

Mediated representations of female offending

Despite the fact that women historically and contemporaneously commit less crime than men (Heidensohn, 1996; Wykes, 1998), Heidensohn (2002) argues that women who do offend, particularly those who engage in violent offences, provide the media with some of the most compelling imaginings of crime and deviancy. Crime news reporting is one of the key ways in which the public receive information about deviancy, criminality and law and order (Chibnall, 1977; Critcher, 2003; Machado and Santos, 2009). Despite the public not being totally passive receivers of information (Ericson et al, 1991), the news media conveys a plethora of detail about crime and is often the public's main source of information about the issue (Feilezer, 2007). However, in spite of this potential moral responsibility, media tends to favour certain types of crime stories over others (Jewkes, 2015; Kitzinger, 2004; Cohen, 1972; Graber, 1980). Jewkes (2015) suggests that through the process of agenda setting, media professionals sift and select news items, prioritise some news stories over others and decide the overall tone of a news story. She suggests that this collectively works to convey stories in a particular way, thus providing certain pictures of the world, which help to structure the audience's frames of reference. Both the media and the public are fascinated by female criminality, due to its rarity and its conflict with the stereotypes of traditional femininity (Berrington and Honkatukia, 2002). Myers and Wight (1996) argue that when a woman offends, her sex is the principal factor through which all of her actions are seen and understood. They suggest that the sensationalised reporting of women's violence in particular can be viewed as a sign of social anxiety about women's roles and the demise of traditional femininity.

The implied biological and pathological difference of female offenders (in comparison to male counterparts) has been argued to lead to their differential treatment in legal and media contexts. The chivalry hypothesis argues that women offenders receive more lenient sentences in criminal cases, because they are viewed as being weak and irrational within the context of the law (Adler, 1975). However, Lloyd (1995) argues that this sort of treatment is only extended to a certain type of female offender, namely those who mostly adhere to the patriarchal expectations of womanhood and motherhood (Daly, 1994; Grabe et al, 2006). Women offenders who commit offences which challenge traditional, 'normative' constructions of femininity and womanhood, such as violent acts or murder, are treated and sentenced harshly (Ballinger, 2000; Edwards, 1984).

Grabe et al (2006) explored the journalistic representations of female offenders and tested the chivalry hypothesis within a news media context. They argued that women only received lenient press coverage if their crime did not violate gender stereotypes and, rather, that women who committed violent crimes or crimes against children were particularly harshly represented. They proposed a 'patriarchal hypothesis', which emphasises that it is the type of crime and how it is linked to gender expectations that shapes news coverage, rather than the sex of the offender (Grabe et al, 2006). This highlights the importance of 'normative' constructions of gender and gender performativity (Butler, 1990) when considering how female offenders are represented and constructed, particularly in media discourse. Consequently, female offenders are routinely constructed as being 'doubly deviant, doubly damned' as they have offended both against the criminal law and the informal laws surrounding appropriate femininity and womanhood (Lloyd, 1995; Wykes and Welsh, 2009).

Simplistic and pathological discourses are often utilised in the social construction of female offenders in an attempt to make sense of such offending behaviour, particularly by news media and legal professionals. For example, women offenders are often constructed within the binary of 'mad' or 'bad'. The 'mad' discourse limits explanations of female offending to irrationality and psychological impairment and the 'bad' discourse constructs female offenders to be inherently evil and an antithesis to 'normal' women (Heidensohn, 1996; Ballinger, 2000). Bad women in particular are demonised (Naylor, 2001; Berrington and Honkatukia, 2002), masculinised (Grabe et al, 2006; Barnett, 2006) and chastised for their sexual deviance (Berrington and Honkatukia, 2002). Women's capacity to engage in crime, particularly violent crime, is often linked to their supposed irrationality, emotional tendencies, madness and/or 'badness' in popular narratives (Naylor, 2001; Cavaglion, 2008). The social construction of female offenders often relies on such deterministic and gendered discourses to explain and account for their offending, which consequently minimises the potential for more nuanced and holistic explanations for such behaviour.

Female offending stock narratives

Considering representations of female offenders more closely, Jewkes (2015) argues that there are a number of stock narratives which are used to build an image and particular gendered construction of female offenders. These narratives and motifs form part of the dominant stereotypes and myths surrounding female deviancy and criminality. For example, female offenders are often constructed within gendered narratives of physical attractiveness, particularly in a media context. The media engage in a very particular construction of gender whereby certain aspects of femininity are valued over others, such as youth, slenderness and other such physical characteristics which satisfy the 'male gaze' (Wykes and Gunter, 2005). This is the case in advertising, women's magazines and tabloid newspapers, but it also extends to news discourse surrounding female criminality (Jewkes, 2015; Barlow and Lynes, 2015). According to Jewkes (2015), women cannot win within this narrative. If female offenders are conventionally attractive, they are described as femme fatales who are able to manipulate with their looks, yet if they are conventionally unattractive they are often described as cold, detached and masculine (Jewkes, 2015).

Women offenders are also often categorised as a 'bad mother'. The 'bad mother' motif is so pervasive, it often applies to all female offenders, whether actual mothers or non-mothers and irrespective of whether their crimes involve children (Jewkes, 2015). Even if female offenders do not have children of their own, yet commit a crime involving children, they are deemed guilty of not only breaking the law, but also of breaking every informal cultural and societal expectation of womanhood and motherhood (Jewkes, 2015). Barnett (2006) argues that journalists rely on gendered ideals surrounding 'good motherhood' in stories of women who kill their children in particular. However, the analysis discussed here highlights that the 'bad mother' motif is applicable to a range of criminal offences, extending beyond cases of child murder or those involving child victims more broadly, thus highlighting that discourses surrounding 'motherhood' and 'womanhood' are virtually indistinguishable. Furthermore, considering the previous narratives of 'mad' and 'bad', Naffine (1987) argues that women portrayed as 'mad', yet morally pure, are often viewed as 'good mothers' and their crimes are considered to be uncontrollable, irrational acts, which are usually the result of mental health issues. However, in contrast, women characterised as 'bad' are portrayed as cold, evil mothers, who have been neglectful of their children and domestic responsibilities.

Jewkes (2015) argues that one of the key ways in which women who commit serious crimes are represented in media discourse in particular is as 'mythical monsters', such as witches, Satanists, vampires and 'fallen women'. According to Jewkes (2015), two favoured figures from Greek mythology which are used to describe female offenders are Medea and Medusa. Medea was an enchantress who, when spurned by her lover, murdered her children, while Medusa was a snake-haired monster who turned her victims to stone with a stare (Jewkes, 2015). Tabloid newspapers have made use of both symbolic figures in the coverage of Myra Hindley (convicted with her partner, Ian Brady, of murdering five children between 1963–65), particularly via the usage of imagery

(Birch, 1993; Boyle, 2005). Birch (1993) argues that due to the media's distinct and purposeful usage of imagery during the reporting of Myra Hindley's case, particularly the use of the now infamous mugshot, the image of her dyed blonde hair and impassive stare, connotes 'modern affectless evil in a way that the contemporary photograph of Brady never has' (French, 1996: 38). By comparing female offenders to mythical monsters in this way, the media ignite society's darkest fears about women, which subsequently become interconnected with folk tales about supernatural monsters, thus transforming such women into almost fictional caricatures of themselves (Jewkes, 2015).

The final stock narrative, which is particularly relevant to this analysis is the 'evil manipulator' (Jewkes, 2015). This description echoes Pollack's (1950) theory, which suggests that women are inherently deceitful. In her analysis of the media coverage of the triple homicide at Orderud Farm, Skilbrei (2013) suggests that the two sisters involved, Kristen and Veronica, were represented as being 'femme fatales' who manipulated their male partners/accomplices to become involved in the murders. Skilbrei (2013) demonstrates that although the femme fatale narrative can be utilised in such instances to portray the women as being powerful and in control of their lives, it simultaneously categorises them as manipulators who are able to use their femininity to pursue deviancy. Furthermore, Jewkes (2015) suggests that this narrative is particularly applicable to women who commit criminal acts alongside their male lover/partner. Jewkes (2015: 128) argues that 'women who form murderous alliances with men are the most problematic for the institutions that seek to understand them and communicate their actions to the rest of society'. Morrisey (2003) suggests that such female offenders represent an enigma to mainstream academics, mainly because it is often difficult to ascertain their role and culpability.

Representations of female and male co-offending

The representation of women who commit crime with a male partner has received relatively little scholarly attention (Grabe et al, 2006).

As highlighted by Morrisey (2003) the construction of such criminal partnerships are difficult to comprehend, as the women involved do not always readily fit within the pre-established narratives. Although the men within the partnership are often presented as evil, the women are portrayed as being instrumental in unleashing the violence and depravity that the man has thus far contained (Jewkes, 2015). The archetypal female–male partnership in recent crime history could be argued to be Myra Hindley and her partner, Ian Brady. Despite Brady being the 'mastermind' in the offending, Hindley's culpability is regarded with greater societal anxiety and disdain (Jewkes, 2015; Jones and Wardle, 2008). Although some critics argue that women like Hindley seek out equally depraved men because they have similar desires (Morrisey, 2003), others argue that such women fall under the influence of controlling men and would not have become involved in such offences were it not for his influence (Richie, 1996; Wykes, 1998; Welle and Falkin, 2000). Despite such conclusions being made within academia, women are often socially constructed as being either equal accomplices (Jones and Wardle, 2008) or more culpable than their male accomplice (Kirsta, 1994) within instances of female–male co-offending.

In addition, Jones and Wardle (2008) suggest that the visual construction of female co-offenders is also particularly significant to their wider representation. They argued that the visual construction of Maxine Carr in the news media represented her in such a way that she was portrayed as being an equal accomplice to her male partner and co-offender, Ian Huntley, despite her unequal involvement. Jones and Wardle (2008: 64) cite the following example from *The Daily Mail* (2003d), which detailed the following quote, said by Huntley, in the headline 'I picked Jessica up, took her downstairs and went back for Holly. I put the bodies in my car and drove.' However, to the immediate right of the headline is a large colour image of Carr, therefore the visual construction of this article implies that it was in fact Carr, not Huntley, who played the larger role in the criminal offences (Jones and Wardle, 2008). This demonstrates that irrespective of the role that Carr actually played in the murder of Holly Wells and Jessica Chapman, her involvement in the crime was enough to demonise her and construct her as being an equal accomplice to her partner, Ian Huntley. Consequently, the extent of Carr's offending was exaggerated to reinforce pre-existing notions of 'feminine evil' (Jones and Wardle, 2008).

Furthermore, in their analysis of the news media's usage of the 'chivalry hypothesis', Grabe et al (2006) found that when women committed crimes which violated society's expected gender norms, they received harsher journalistic treatment than men who committed similar crimes. Furthermore, they discussed what they coined the 'Bonnie and Clyde effect', which suggests that stories about men and women collaborating in crime are often associated with harsher journalistic treatment than stories about men and women acting without each other's support (Grabe et al, 2006). They suggest that a potential reason as to why gender collaboration in crime received more sensational coverage is because that it deviates from behavioural expectations of both genders, 'doubling the potential for journalistic titillation' (Grabe et al, 2006: 159).

Overall, the construction of female–male co-offending has received little scholarly attention, particularly when considering both a legal and media context. However, existing research suggests that due to difficulties in trying to explain the phenomena, journalists often use overly simplistic narratives to explain such offending, thus leading to its misrepresentation and a consequent failure to understand the novel and unique features of this type of criminality.

Conclusion

Women are represented and constructed in stereotypical ways, often using gendered motifs, in media and public discourse more broadly (Ross, 2007; Carter and Steiner, 2004). The representation of female offenders in legal and media discourse is largely confined to restrictive and essentialist narratives, such as 'mad' and 'bad' (Lloyd, 1995; Jewkes, 2015). Depending on the nature of their crime, female offenders can occasionally be represented somewhat sympathetically if their acts of violence or criminality can be explained by hormones, irrationality and/or 'madness'. However, for typically non-female crimes, such as crimes against children or violent acts, a range of linguistic and discursive techniques are utilised to emphasise the extent to which the women have deviated from 'normal' femininity and womanhood.

The representation of co-offending women has received relatively little scholarly attention, yet existing literature suggests that women co-offenders are routinely represented as 'equal accomplices' (Jones and Wardle, 2008) or in some cases, the woman is often portrayed as being more dangerous than their male counterpart (Kirsta, 1994). The representation of women within such partnerships is particularly interesting to consider, as initial research suggests that they often receive much harsher journalistic coverage than their male counterpart, irrespective of their level of involvement in the criminality (Barlow, 2015b; Grabe et al, 2006; Jones and Wardle, 2008), thus further highlighting the gendered nature of the social construction of female (co)offending.

TWO
THEORETICAL UNDERSTANDINGS OF COERCION AS A PATHWAY INTO CRIME

Introduction

This chapter will begin by exploring women's pathways into crime, before specifically considering coercion as a pathway into crime for female co-offenders. It will critically discuss concepts such as agency and 'choice' within the context of such relationships/co-offending partnerships. The chapter will conclude with a critical overview of criminology's current engagement with and understanding of coerced women.

Pathways into crime for women offenders

Literature exploring pathways into crime has been widely criticised for devoting insufficient attention to female offenders. Feminist scholars in particular question whether theories developed by men about men can account for women's experiences (Daly and Chesney-Lind, 1988). However, from the 1970s onwards, a body of research collectively termed 'feminist pathways' research sought to explain why and how women become entrenched in the criminal justice system

(Belknap, 2007). This body of work produced compelling narratives of women offenders and identified key issues, risks and experiences characterising women's pathways into crime. Significantly, these factors appeared to be qualitatively different to those of male offenders (for example, Belknap, 2007; Chesney-Lind and Shelden, 2004; Daly, 1994; Richie, 1996).

Pathways into crime for women offenders identified within this body of research includes childhood victimisation, which proposes causal links between serious child abuse, mental health issues and female offending behaviour (Covington, 1988; Daly, 1994). In addition, the extreme marginalisation pathway identified a pattern of poverty, homelessness and educational issues and emphasised the significance of the intersection of race, gender and class among certain women offenders (Richie, 1996). Perhaps most pertinent to this book is the identification of a relational pathway, which identified a combination of dysfunctional relationships, adult victimisation and in some instances substance abuse as playing a central role in women's offending decisions and behaviour (Gilligan, 1982).

Daly's (1994) research most strongly encapsulates the feminist pathways perspective and she identified five pathways into crime for women. She labelled each identified pathway as follows: (a) street women – this usually involved women or girls escaping abuse and violence, entering street life and often engaging in sex work, drugs and theft to survive; (b) drug-connected women – this involved women using and trafficking drugs, often with intimate partners or family members; (c) harmed and harming women – these were women who had experienced physical and/or child sex abuse and neglect, school delinquency issues, drug use and displayed an overall hostile demeanour; (d) battered women – these were women who had suffered abuse within the context of an adult, intimate relationship, which is consequently connected to offending behaviour; (e) 'other' women – this group consisted of women who were not particularly disadvantaged, but were rather motivated by greed and their offending usually involved economic gain. Daly's (1994) work is among a growing body of research, which recognises the significance and high rates of victimisation that links violence in women's lives to their offending and their subsequent entry into the criminal justice system (Chesney-Lind, 1997; Katz, 2000; Richie, 1996). Such research increasingly recognises the potential impact and influence of co-offending with a male partner on women's pathways into crime and reasons for offending (Richie, 1996; Welle and Falkin, 2000).

Co-offending and coercion

The act of committing crime alongside one or more accomplices has received relatively little criminological attention (Carrington, 2002; Warr, 1996). Relatively few studies of co-offending exist and the majority are restricted to juvenile samples (McGloin et al, 2008), male offenders (Reiss and Farrington, 1991) and particular crimes, for example, violence (Pettersson, 2005). However, research is increasingly recognising the potential impact of co-offending relationships, particularly within the context of women's criminality. Becker and McCorkel (2011) argue that women are more likely to engage in gender atypical offences when they co-offend with men, such as robbery and murder. Furthermore, Mullins and Wright (2003) suggest that women are often introduced to offences, such as residential burglary, by an intimate male partner. Koons-Witt and Schram (2003) argued that although women who commit crimes alone are more likely to be involved in aggravated assaults, those who co-offend with men often commit more serious offences. Moreover, there has been substantial support for the idea that in specific instances of co-offending, men can *coerce* women to commit a criminal act. Coercion is defined here as the action or practice of persuading, forcing or encouraging someone to do something (such as commit a criminal act) by using force, threats, abuse of emotion and/or control.

The phenomenon of being coerced has been found in certain types of offending partnerships. For example, Avelardo (2007) and Brown (2007) both argued that female gang members can be coerced into crime by male gang members, particularly if they are in an intimate relationship. Brown (2007) argued that many young female gang members are frequently forced to hoard drugs or take the blame for criminal offences on their partner's behalf. Furthermore, research suggests that the relationship between 'pimps' and female sex workers can be characterised by coercion. Kennedy et al (2007) argued that if female sex-workers are 'managed' or controlled by a male 'pimp', they can control many, if not all, aspects of the female sex workers' lives, for example, managing their money and getting them involved in drugs. This leads to such women perceiving that they have few life choices and many therefore remain within the sex industry. It is not the suggestion here that all female sex workers are coerced into the industry, as many do so with agency and choice (Sanders et al, 2009), but those whose work is controlled by a male pimp may experience coercion and control within the context of this relationship (Kennedy et al, 2007). In addition, it has also been suggested that women who sexually abuse their own and/or other people's children alongside their male partner can be coerced to become involved in the activity by a male partner or accomplice (Syed and Williams, 1996). Matthews et al (1991) categorised female sex offenders and found that 'male coerced women' tended to view their relationship with their partner as more important than the wellbeing of the child victim. Furthermore, the male-coerced women in the study were usually extremely dependent on their male partner and the men often encouraged them to believe that their co-offending was an integral part of their relationship. This collectively suggests that in certain types of co-offending relationships, women can be coerced into illegal activity by their male partner/accomplice, particularly if they are involved in an intimate, personal relationship together.

A relatively small amount of research has explored the nature of the personal relationship between male and female co-offenders. Welle and Falkin (2000) argue that women who have a 'romantic' relationship with their male co-defendant are more vulnerable to manipulation and coercion and often experience isolation and threats within this intimate relationship. Such women experienced what Welle and Falkin (2000) coined 'relationship policing', as they often became involved in crime due to their fear of disappointing or disobeying their partner as opposed to making a fully 'rational' decision to participate. The authors concluded that 'women with romantic co-defendants experienced a continuum of policing, in which abusive partners police women both at home and in public' (2000: 61).

Furthermore, Richie's (1996) exploration of African American women's experiences of being forced into crime by their male partner could also be applicable to a variety of coercive, intimate relationships. For instance, Richie (1996) suggests that the notion of 'gender entrapment' 'helps to show how some women are forced or coerced into crime by their culturally expected gender roles, the violence in their intimate relationships and their social position in the broader society' (1996: 133). Richie (1996) suggests that this concept helps to highlight why African American women stay in relationships characterised by coercion and abuse. Such women often place greater emphasis on family loyalty and keeping their relationship together, rather than their own wellbeing and personal safety. The women experienced violence and oppression in both their private lives, in the form of abuse, violence and control, as well as in public, due to experiences of racism, their low socio-economic status and marginalisation within society more broadly. Richie (1996) argues that this combination of oppressions led the women to be 'compelled' into a variety of illegal activities.

In addition, Jones (2008) suggested that male and female co-offending relationships could be classified in various ways, for example, women who were in a coercive relationship with their partner, women who committed a crime through love and women who were 'equal' partners in their criminality. Jones (2008) argued that it was the nature of the personal relationship between the male and female co-defendants which determined why the women became involved in criminal activity. He recognised that although some women may make a 'rational' decision or an informed choice to offend, others are forced to do so by their controlling and abusive partners. Jones concluded that the high level of both mental and physical coercion reported by the women suggests that a substantial amount of female offending may be explicable on this basis (2008: 160). Furthermore, in later research, Jones (2011) argued that the coercive nature of such relationships helped to explain why many female prisoners had pleaded guilty to a crime that they had not committed, due to an excessive desire to protect their partner's needs above their own or alternatively, because that they were coerced to do so by their male co-offender.

Perhaps the most interesting aspect of Jones' (2008) research are the issues raised around committing a crime due to 'love' or 'fear' of one's partner. In Jones' (2008) research, women who committed a crime out of 'love' or enthrallment and those who committed a crime out of fear could be separated into two, distinct categories defined by the kind of abuse that the women experienced. For example, Jones (2008) appears to suggest that because the women in the 'love' category experienced little, if any, physical violence by their male partner, they were not directly forced into crime. However, rather than dichotomising these experiences, an alternative way of understanding this notion is to consider love and fear as part of a continuum of coercive pathways into crime. Whether the women reported committing a crime out of love or fear, both groups argued that they engaged in illegal activity to avoid disappointing or angering their partner. This notion is particularly applicable to the four women analysed in this book, as they each expressed differing levels of suggested coercion, which were collectively characterised by a combination of *both* love and fear. With this in mind, it could be argued that irrespective of whether the women committed a crime out of fear or infatuation/love, both experiences could be viewed as coercive behaviour.

The binary of agency and coercion

A key issue with much existing criminological engagement with coercion as a pathway into crime is the tendency to dichotomise coerced women's experiences. Examples include the categorisation of such women's reasons for committing a criminal act (Jones, 2008) or the simplistic binary of agency and coercion in much of the academic literature. Agency, or the choice to act in a particular way, is often viewed to be in stark contrast or opposition to coercion within existing criminological thought, which thus restricts the social construction of coerced women as either victim or agent.

Feminists have challenged the perception that women are less capable of rationality, reflection and responsibility than men, with many attacking the presumption that men are rational agents while women are not (Morrisey, 2003). Maher argues that, 'the positioning of women as victims constitutes an enduring stumbling block for feminist theory' (1997: 11), because it denies women agency. This highlights that as well as criminology more broadly having difficulties explaining and encapsulating the experiences of coerced women, this also extends to some feminist perspectives. Some scholars (such as Morrisey, 2003) suggest that women offenders should be viewed as autonomous individuals *choosing* to commit crime as a conscious and deliberate act, in other words, exercising agency. In such situations, it is entirely inappropriate to suggest a defence of 'diminished responsibility' simply by virtue of being women. However other scholars have argued that female offenders have different motivations to commit crime, as some women may be influenced by issues such as personal circumstance, poverty or coercion (Carlen, 1988; Ballinger, 2000; Richie, 1996). It is therefore crucial to appreciate the specific contexts within which women commit crime, so as to develop a more nuanced understanding of women's offending behaviour.

Furthermore, Maher (1997) suggests that female offenders are typically viewed to be either wholly independent agents or as being 'out of control' of their offending behaviour. However, this dichotomisation of agency is a reductionist approach and does not apply to all female offending behaviour, as highlighted by the four case studies of co-accused women discussed here. The binary categorisation of agency and coercion leads to over-simplistic understandings of coerced women's perspectives, which often fail to encapsulate their lived experiences. However, as argued by Madhok et al (2013: 3) when discussing the binary of coercion and agency: 'If we can have only one or the other, then repudiating patronising images of the oppressed and powerless requires us to deny, or at least obscure, the extent to which social relations of inequality and domination continue to structure our lives.'

This highlights the ways in which the emphasis on individual, 'rational' choice and autonomy within existing definitions of agency serve to minimise experiences of coercion and the ways in which deep-rooted, societal gender inequality and oppression have an impact on women's pathways into crime (Carlen, 1988; Ballinger, 2000; Heidensohn, 2002). It is the aim of this book to move away from solely focusing on individual capacities and vulnerabilities when considering co-offending women's pathways into crime and to explore the potential influence of wider power regimes and social inequalities. With this in mind, when attempting to understand coerced women's experiences and pathways into crime, this book endeavours to shift the focus away from simple binaries of 'agent' or 'victim' and to consider the complex ways in which agency and coercion are entwined – 'a dynamic continuum of simultaneity' (Madhok et al, 2013: 3).

Context and contribution

With all of this in mind, existing feminist pathways literature is yet to specifically explore female co-offenders' pathways into crime (Daly, 1994) and much of the broader co-offending literature focuses on specific types of co-offending partnerships (for example Brown, 2007; Matthews et al, 1991) or places co-offending women's reasons for offending into simplistic categories (Jones, 2008). Furthermore, academic literature has yet to explore the social construction of coercion as a pathway into crime. With this in mind, this book aims to consider the media, legal and broader social construction of coercion as a pathway into crime for co-offending women and to develop a nuanced conceptual and theoretical framework of coercion as a pathway into crime. To do so, four case studies of co-accused women will be critically analysed in Chapters Four and Five. The next chapter will consider the methodological approach used in this research and discuss the benefits of such techniques for criminologists and social researchers.

THREE
UNDERSTANDING THE SOCIAL CONSTRUCTION OF COERCED WOMEN

Introduction

This chapter will outline the feminist methodology deployed in the analysis of the case studies, which involved adopting a woman-centred approach to research and aims to gain a more nuanced understanding of the co-accused women's experiences and stories (Letherby, 2003). The chapter will also discuss the benefits of using a case study approach in criminological research and will critically consider the strengths and limitations of this particular method. Finally, the chapter will identify the sources of data used, that is, newspaper articles and case and court file documents, which are used as a comparative/corroborative tool, as well as discussing the feminist framework developed for analysis. The chapter will conclude with a discussion of the benefits of using a similar approach to data collection and analysis in other criminological research.

Feminist methodological approach

This book adopts a feminist methodological approach, which involves advocating a woman-centred approach to research (Letherby, 2003). A feminist methodology involves adopting a methodological position which does not 'add' women to research, but rather attempts to gain a more nuanced understanding of their experiences. As highlighted by Cook and Fonow (1990: 80) 'feminist research is thus, not research about women but research for women to be used in transforming their sexist society'. With this in mind, the ways in which the co-offending women's experiences and voices have been constructed and interpreted by journalists and legal professionals is explored here, which reveals insights into the assumptions that such constructions encourage us to make about female offenders more broadly. A feminist methodological approach also considers critical reflexivity as being an integral aspect of the research process and this study recognises the significance of researcher subjectivity and positionality (Stanley and Wise, 1993; Oakley, 1992; England, 1994; Mosselson, 2010; Letherby, 2003). It is argued here that a more reflexive approach to research and acknowledging the influence of researcher positionality and emotions, arguably produces stronger objectivity within research and signals its manifest subjectivity (Harding, 1991; Barlow, 2015a).

Case study approach

A case study method is utilised, using four cases of women who have been co-accused with their male partner (accomplice/s) of committing a range of crimes. Using a case study approach allows the researcher to fully engage with the cultural contexts and lived realities of those researched (Ferrell et al, 2004). Following the example of Yin (2009), this research uses multiple sources of data and adopts an embedded multiple case design to improve data triangulation and internal validity. Using a multiple case design is a more robust and rigorous method in comparison to adopting a single case study design (Herriott and Firestone, 1983). Yin (2009) argues that analytic conclusions that have arisen from two or more cases are more powerful than those coming from a single case. The case study analytical technique used within this research was cross case synthesis. This technique initially treats each case as an individual case study and subsequently, the overlapping themes across each of the cases are explored and analysed (Yin, 2009).

Although using a case study approach has been criticised due to its perceived lack of rigour and generalisability, Yin (2009) argues that the aim of case study research is to expand and generalise theories, not to enumerate frequencies. Furthermore, Flyvbjerg (2006: 226) argues that 'formal generalization, whether on the basis of large samples or single cases, is considerably overrated as the main source of scientific progress' and the emphasis should instead be on the quality of the research. Thomas (2010) also suggests that such weaknesses of the case study method are not disguised, yet other design frames in social science which seek ways of calibrating and enabling generalisation suggest the applicability of their study to other settings, when in fact generalisability is not always guaranteed. Furthermore, Yin (2009) argues that to suggest that findings from case study research are not transferable to other cases or contexts is not an accurate reflection of reality. With this in mind, although this research does not attempt to be generalisable in the scientific sense, it is argued that the wide-range of criminal offences committed in the cases analysed, the breadth of data and in-depth analysis enhances the replicability of the findings to other cases.

Additionally, case study methods are often criticised for containing bias towards verification, that is, a tendency to confirm the researchers' preconceived notions. However, Flyvbjerg (2006) suggests that the question of subjectivism and bias applies to all methods, not just the case study. Furthermore, Beveridge (1951) concludes that there are more discoveries stemming from the intense observation made possible by case studies than from statistics applied to large groups, which highlights the potential value of this method.

With this in mind, using a case study approach in criminological research has a number of advantages. For example, it enables the opportunity to fully engage with the lives of those being researched, it allows the researcher to draw upon a range of documents and sources to draw conclusions and it also enables cross case comparisons to strengthen findings. This method is particularly useful when researching a hard to reach sample group, such as those involved in high profile cases, which often have a wealth of accessible secondary sources available for analysis. Rather than dismissing the case study method due to its perceived lack of generalisability and suggested susceptibility to subjectivity, the depth and breadth of knowledge that can be gained from this method should be acknowledged and utilised by criminologists.

The case studies used here were selected as they are each high profile examples of co-accused women which have occurred within the last 15 years, therefore they received extensive media attention, which generated a viable volume of news coverage to analyse. In addition, the crimes committed range in severity and offence type, thus enabling a critical analysis of whether the nature of the crime influences the women's construction and representation. A Privileged Access Agreement (PAA) granted by Her Majesty's Court and Tribunal Services (HMCTS) enabled the access to the case and court file material. The case file documents were not publically available and were therefore a source of material which very few people, other than those who were in attendance during the trials, would ever have access to. With this in mind, as part of the terms and conditions of the PAA, it was required that in any published material which discussed the cases and court file data, all details related to the cases, including names of offenders, victims and places, would need to be anonymised. The PAA recognised that full anonymity would be virtually impossible to achieve due to the high profile nature of the cases, yet it was stated that confidentiality should be adhered to 'as far as possible' (PAA, 2012: 4). As a result of this, pseudonyms were provided for all individuals involved in the case studies analysed. Consequently, the basic and required information about the cases has been provided, but an in-depth overview was not possible. Furthermore, many of the documents within the case file material were not dated or numbered, however as much detail as possible and appropriate titles are provided throughout subsequent chapters.

The case studies analysed are *Jane Turner, Sarah Johnson, Alice Jones* and *Janet Young*, all of whom were accused of committing a range of crimes with a male partner. Jane Turner was a nursery worker, who was involved in the exchange of indecent imagery of children via an online paedophile ring. She was eventually convicted and sentenced in 2009. At the time of her conviction, Jane was 40 years of age and married with two children. She had no previous offending history. Jane met one of her accomplices, *Simon*, on a social networking site, where Simon eventually began to talk about his sexual interest in young children. Jane admits to being 'obsessed' with Simon and she eventually agreed to take indecent images of children at the nursery where she worked and sent the photographs to him online, in exchange for 'love' and attention. Also involved in the online network was Susan, who took pictures of herself abusing a child and sent them to Simon. Simon had recruited two other women to his 'paedophile network', *Louise* and *Tracey*, who also took indecent images of themselves abusing children and sent them to Simon. Although Jane and Susan knew about each other, they rarely communicated and neither knew about Louise or Tracey until after their arrest. Simon was the first member of the network to be arrested and Jane and Susan were arrested shortly afterwards. The three went on trial together, but following the emergence of the images sent by Louise and Tracey a few weeks later, Simon was sentenced the following year alongside the two women. Jane received a minimum sentence of seven years, Simon nine years, Susan five years, Louise seven years and Tracey four years.

Sarah Johnson was convicted for perverting the course of justice in a child murder case in 2003. Her partner, *David Fox*, was charged with the murder of two schoolchildren (*Lucy* and *Katie*) in 2002 and was found guilty in December 2003, when he was sentenced to life imprisonment for their murder. Sarah Johnson was initially charged with two counts of assisting an offender, but was cleared of these offences and was found guilty of conspiring to pervert the course of justice. Sarah was 22 years old at the time of the offence and had no previous offending history. She provided a false alibi for David on the night that the two girls were murdered, but she insisted throughout the trial that she did not believe, at any point, that David had murdered them. She received a three-and-a-half year prison sentence.

Alice Jones was convicted of a range of fraudulent offences in 2007, as she helped her husband fake his own death (in March 2002). Alice was aged 53 at the time of the offence and had two adult sons with her husband *Chris*. Alice had no previous offending history. The Jones' argued that this decision was due to the extensive and mounting debt that they were experiencing. Significantly, the Jones' sons, family and friends did not know the truth about Chris' fabricated disappearance. Alice Jones secured a death certificate for Chris and was thus able to claim his life insurance funds, pension and various other financial gains. In 2007, following Chris' confession to the police, both Chris and Alice admitted that they had been involved in the fraud and they were both charged with various fraud charges, including: obtaining money by deception, money laundering, transferring and converting criminal property. While Chris pleaded guilty to the 15 charges he faced, Alice Jones pleaded not guilty to all of her charges and suggested that she had been coerced by Chris to be involved in the offending, citing the defence of 'marital coercion'. Alice Jones was eventually found guilty of 13 counts of fraud and deception and was sentenced to six-and-a-half years' imprisonment and Chris Jones was sentenced to six years and three months' imprisonment.

Finally, in 2011, Janet was interviewed by police officers over allegations that in 2003, she had accepted driving licence penalty points actually incurred by her then husband, *Edward Crouch*. This transpired as Janet disclosed to the British Press in 2011 that Edward had forced an unnamed individual to take his penalty points. This incident, coincidently or not, followed a public divorce between the couple following Edward's disclosure of an affair. Despite aiming to remain anonymous, it eventually emerged that it was Janet who had taken the penalty points on her husband's behalf. In 2012, both Janet and Edward were charged with perverting the course of justice. At the time of her arrest, Janet was 62 years old and she had no previous offending history. Janet entered a plea of not guilty and cited the defence of marital coercion at trial. Initially, Edward also pleaded not guilty, but eventually admitted to his involvement in the offence prior to going to trial. In March 2013, Edward and Janet were convicted of perverting the course of justice and both were sentenced to eight months' imprisonment.

Using documents in criminological research

Documents are increasingly recognised as being insightful and rich data sources dispelling the notion that they are a dry and dull data source. For example, Steedman (2001; 2013) emphasises the romance of archival data, highlighting the beauty in 'letting someone else's words move through my head and hand and onto my own bit of paper' (Steedman, 2013: 27). This highlights that both the practical and romantic considerations in reading archival data are increasingly recognised and valued. However, documents are not viewed as such rich and valuable sources of data within criminological research and are often viewed as being of secondary significance and epistemic privilege in comparison to primary data sources. Furthermore, debates are yet to move forward with regard to concerns such as negotiating access to restricted documents, considering the emotional risk of using certain types of document in research and the consequent (at least potential) impact on the researcher's emotional health (with the exception of Barlow, 2015a).

The documents used in the case studies analysed here were newspaper articles and case and court file documents were used as a comparative tool. The case and court file documents provided a means of exploring journalistic processes of selection, exclusion and emphasis. This combination of sources is a novel methodological approach, particularly when using contemporary documents rather than historical/archival data. Comparing and contrasting the courtroom and newspaper 'versions' of the same events show the ways in which they differ, particularly highlighting journalists' propensity to focus on specific aspects of criminal acts. As highlighted by Surette (1998), the media and legal system should not be viewed as autonomous entities and instead, the complex interactions and relationship between them should be closely examined. Furthermore, comparing newspaper articles with case file analysis revealed useful insights as to the extent to which the co-accused women's testimonies and voices were heard or rendered invisible in news media content. Using the case file documents as a corroborative tool therefore produced a more inclusive account of the women's stories and enabled their voices to be listened to and heard, albeit only partially.

A selection of both daily and Sunday publications were analysed, with a combination of broadsheet and tabloid newspaper titles. Broadsheet newspapers present themselves as providing serious news and usually have longer articles, whereas tabloids typically focus on entertainment value and the 'human interest factor' and often have shorter articles for quick reading (Franklin, 2003; Cole and Harcup, 2010). The following newspapers (along with their Sunday published versions) were selected for analysis, as they are among the highest circulation newspapers in the UK and due to their differences in ideological leanings: *Daily Mail, Daily Telegraph, The Guardian, The Independent, The Express, The Mirror, The Sun, The Times.*

Each of the co-accused women case studies occurred between 2003 and 2013 and all news articles related to each of the four case studies were analysed from when the co-defendants were accused and arrested, through to two weeks following their sentences and/or appeals (where applicable). This timeframe was chosen, as it allowed useful comparisons to be made between the court and case file documents and the newspaper articles. Furthermore, the time period of analysis was extended to two weeks following the sentencing for the news articles, so that any stories which were published after the verdict had been announced could also be analysed.

As well as using newspaper data, this research also analyses the portrayal of the co-accused women during their trials, by using the case and court file documents as a comparative tool. Following a rigorous application process, a PAA was granted by HMCTS, which provided a unique opportunity to access the case and court file material of the trials of the four co-accused women. A vast range of documents were included within each of the case files, including police interview transcripts, prosecution and defence arguments, sections of the trial transcripts and judges' opening and closing statements. However, it is significant to note that the documents within the case file material were stored at the conclusion of the trials by the court clerks, rather than being selected for the purpose of this study. In spite of this, court clerks are encouraged to store all material relating to the trial and fortunately, each of the case files contained a vast range of documents, as previously discussed. Another relevant observation of the case file material is that each of the available trial transcripts were 'snapshots' that were transcribed for a specific purpose external to this research, for example, due to the perceived significance to the case. However, although it is useful to acknowledge the potential context in which these transcripts were obtained and used during the case, the insights that they provided, particularly in terms of how the co-accused women were represented during their trials and how they discussed their experiences during their testimonies, were invaluable to the research.

In addition, exploring legal discourse is advantageous as it could provide insights into how legal and sentencing decisions are made and by whom during criminal case proceedings. Furthermore, in-depth analysis of legal discourse can reveal interesting observations about *why* decisions could have been made, as well as exploring how offenders are constructed during case proceedings. Feminist theorists have noted that the law holds a symbolic superiority in the production of knowledge and truth (Inglis, 2003), owing to its claim to be objective, value free and apolitical (Ballinger, 2011: 109). It has been argued that the law is constructed according to male values, thus taken for granted legal terms, such as the 'reasonable man of the law', are socially constructed according to the characteristics of masculinity (Smart, 1989; Ballinger, 2012). Exploring the legal representation of the co-accused women through a 'feminist lens' (Ballinger, 2000; 2012) encourages a critical consideration about the predominantly male-defined legal process, thus allowing a more nuanced understanding of the women's perspectives and the ways in which they were marginalised or ignored.

Conclusion

In conclusion, the feminist methodology (Harding, 1987; Letherby, 2003) and case study approach (Yin, 2009) utilised here enabled an in-depth understanding of the women's experiences, perspectives and stories. The experiences of women co-offenders, such as those analysed in this research, are mainly discussed through the lens of the media, thus offering a partial and at times distorted view of their version of events. However, by considering the gendered ways in which they are constructed and the potential consequences of this, this book aims to offer a more authentic account of their experiences.

Furthermore, documents are a useful source of data in criminological research and analysing both the news media and case file data in the current research produced a more nuanced understanding of journalistic practice and the ways in which the women's perspectives were reinterpreted, silenced and mostly ignored in both the court proceedings and media discourse. It is argued here that a similar methodological approach could be utilised in other criminological research, which will enable a more nuanced insight into the ways in which the media represent, interpret and construct offenders and criminal cases more broadly.

FOUR
A FEMINIST CRITIQUE OF REPRESENTATIONS OF POTENTIALLY COERCED WOMEN

Introduction

This chapter will discuss the media construction of women co-offenders and their relationship with their male partner/co-offender, using the case and court file material as a comparative tool. It will particularly consider the ways in which the women's representation served to minimise and discredit their perspectives and defence, particularly in relation to the potential influence of their relationship with their male partner on their offending behaviour. It will also consider the ways in which the women's suggestions of coercion or coercive techniques (at varying levels) by their male partner were constructed, particularly in media discourse. In doing so, the chapter will be divided into a number of key themes, such as 'bad women' and 'equally bad or worse'. It is important to note that the themes apply to the women at varying levels and the extent to which they were evident in the women's legal and media representation will be discussed.

'Bad women': influence of gendered discourses

Victorian discourses of the feminine ideal and womanhood, namely domesticity, respectability, sexuality and motherhood still have significance even today, particularly when applied to female offenders (Smart, 1976; Ballinger, 2000). The discourses surrounding the feminine ideal suggest that women should be passive, selfless, physically attractive and inherently nurturing (Friedan, 1963; Ballinger, 2000). Female offenders, by their very nature, often contradict such ideals. With this in mind, this section will consider the ways in which gendered assumptions and deviations against femininity served to construct the women as 'bad', particularly drawing on motifs such as 'sexual deviant', 'bad mother' and 'mythical monster'. The potential consequences of this, such as the silencing of the women's perspectives, will also be critically considered.

'Bad mother'

The definition of 'womanhood' as being directly connected to being a mother or desiring to be a mother remains to be a powerful force in women's lives. Ideals of motherhood such as the 'good mother' (Villani and Ryan, 1997) appear to leave little room for anything beyond the possibility of motherhood. The good mother is idealised as being completely selfless, a natural protector of her children and having a great deal of tolerance (Naylor, 2001). Such discourses surrounding the image of the 'good mother' and the antithesis of the 'bad mother' played an integral role in the representation of the co-offending women, particularly Jane Turner, Janet Young and Alice Jones.

Jane was represented as a 'bad mother', due to the neglect of her own children, but also the abuse of her in loco parentis role as a nursery worker. First, Jane was portrayed as a neglectful mother, who invested more time and energy into her online relationship and depraved sexual lifestyle, than in being a mother to her two children. Integral to this neglectful mother narrative was the suggestion that she had transformed from a loving mother, who took good care of her family, to a woman who neglected all of the duties expected of a good mother. This is evidenced in the following quotes:

> She was once the normal average mum. We did baking and cooking together. (Daughter's witness statement, June 2009)

> There was nothing at home being done, I mean nothing: it was untidy, washing that hadn't been done or washing that was done but wasn't put away and it was starting to look really run down. (Quote from Jane's husband, transcript used in documentary, October 2010)

> The once hands-on, loving mother had developed a sinister obsession, which would take her away from her husband and daughters. She neglected every aspect of family life. (Jane, trial transcript, October 2009)

This transformation seemed to be particularly difficult for legal professionals to understand, as this implies that she had the capability to be the good mother that she was expected to be, but instead she actively chose to neglect her duties to satisfy her own sexual depravity.

Furthermore, Jane was referred to as a 'mother of two' or 'mum of two' in a number of news articles (for example, *Daily Mail*, 16 December 2009d; *Express*, 2 October 2009; *Sun*, 11 June 2009a) and quotes from her daughter's highlight that they will 'never call her mum again' and that they think she is 'pure evil' (*Daily Mail*, 5 October 2009c). By using such language, journalists highlight that Jane's crimes against children are twofold, as she harmed her victims at the nursery, but she was also a mother herself, therefore her own children were also victims of the consequences of her crimes. By using her daughters as sources to evidence her incapability as a mother, the news media successfully constructs Jane as a bad mother. This suggested lack of maternal instinct and care for her own children, accompanied by the suggestion that she is 'pure evil', provides a potential explanation for the reader as to how a woman could have committed such crimes, as such descriptions firmly represent her as 'other', who is the antithesis of a good mother and woman.

Jane's transgressions against womanhood were threefold, as not only did she deviate against the expected gender norms of femininity and motherhood, but she also abused her role as a nursery-worker. Jane was in loco parentis for a number of children at the nursery where she worked, therefore her abuse of her position to capture inappropriate images of children was deemed to be a particularly shocking aspect of this case. Within the first two days of the story breaking, Jane was persistently referred to as a 'nursery worker' or 'nursery woman' in a number of headlines. The focus on this identity within the headlines during this time period highlights which aspects of the case the news editor believed to be the most significant and thus reveals important insights into how journalists wanted the crime and case to be perceived.

By referring to Jane in terms of her role (that is, nursery worker), rather than her actual name/who she is, from the beginning of the case, the news media successfully ensured that Jane and her role as a nursery worker became indistinguishable. During later periods of reporting, rather than Jane being referred to as a nursery worker, this changed to her being referenced as a 'nursery paedophile' (*Guardian*, 2 October 2009) or a 'nursery sex monster' (*Mirror*, 16 December 2009c). This demonstrates that as the reporting progressed, Jane was no longer solely defined by her role as a woman, mother or nursery worker and instead, these identities became intertwined with the crimes that she committed. Although this construction was not so evident in the case file material, as Jane was not referenced using emotive terms such as 'paedo' and 'sex monster', legal professionals often used her profession as a nursery worker to evidence the extent to which she had transgressed her gender role expectations, therefore highlighting the significance of such identities in both contexts. This highlights that Jane's construction as a 'bad mother' extended beyond her role as mother to her two daughters, but also her breach of trust in her nursery worker role, thus highlighting the all-encompassing nature of this motif for Jane's broader representation.

The 'bad mother' motif was also evident in the construction of Alice Jones. Both Chris (Alice's husband and co-offender) and Alice lied about Chris' 'faked death' to their sons, which led to them to believe that their father had died. Mothers are expected to be natural nurturers and to put the needs of their children above their own (Smart, 1976; Naylor, 2001), thus any transgression against this ideal leads to the label of the 'bad mother', particularly within the context of offending. With this in mind, irrespective of the fact that Alice's crimes were not committed directly against her sons, as her offences were technically 'victimless' crimes, because they had been hurt and affected in the process, she was subsequently represented as a 'bad mother'. This suggests that Alice was judged not only for her offending, but also for her failure to be a 'good mother' to her sons.

Alice's representation as a 'bad mother' within the context of the trial also appeared to have influenced the sentencing decisions of the judge, as highlighted in the following extract:

> Although the sums involved are not as high as some reported cases, the duration of the offending, its multifaceted nature and in particular the grief inflicted over the years to those who in truth were the real victims, your own sons, whose lives you crushed, make this a case which merits a particularly severe sentence. (Judge's closing speech, 24 July 2008)

This suggests that it was Alice's failure to be a good mother to her sons which was viewed to be the most significant deviant behaviour, rather than her involvement in the fraud itself. Furthermore, during the post sentence write-up (17 August 2008), the Judge elaborated on various points relating to his sentencing decisions. When discussing his reasons for Chris' sentencing, the Judge highlighted that the decision was due to the 'duration' and elaborate nature of the offending, yet for Alice, he stated the following, 'this decision was made due to the duration of the fraud and in particular due to the cruelty she inflicted on her sons' (post sentence report, August 2008). This suggests that idealistic discourses surrounding womanhood and motherhood may in some instances have an impact on the severity and length of sentencing decisions for female offenders, thus exposing the gendered nature of the law (Edwards, 1984; Ballinger, 2000; 2012).

This motif was also evident in the news media material and Alice was directly referred to as 'mother' (115 instances), 'mum' (65) or 'mam' (42) in over half of the articles which mentioned her and significantly, the majority of these articles constructed her as a 'bad mother'. Similar to the case file material, on numerous occasions Alice was openly questioned as a mother:

How could any mother stoop so low? (*Daily Telegraph*, 8 December 2007a)

Across the country, all parents were echoing the same, heart rendering question; how could she? (*People*, 9 December 2007)

Mothers are expected to lie, cheat and perjure themselves in the defence of their sons, and often do, even when those sons are guilty of rape or murder, such a mother would be forgiven by the public more readily than *Alice Jones*. (*Guardian*, 25 July 2008)

The last quote in particular highlights that Alice was judged more readily for the informal and unofficial crimes against her sons, rather than for her actual offending. This therefore suggests that Alice's trial, in both the courtroom and in the media, was twofold, namely for both the fraudulent offences and for being a 'bad mother'.

Furthermore, both legal professionals and journalists in particular placed much less emphasis on Chris' deception of his sons and he was not constructed as a bad father. One of the ways in which journalists reinforced this aspect of the narrative was by using the Jones' sons as sources to evidence Alice's 'bad motherhood':

The wife of *Chris Jones* was flying back to the UK last night to face her two sons, who said they had been left 'astonished' and angry that their mother had let them believe their father had died in a canoe accident when she knew he was alive. (*Guardian*, 6 December 2007)

How could our mam continue to make us believe that our dad had died when he was very much alive? (*Mirror*, 7 December 2007a).

My mam will do anything to save her skin, she lied in court so many times, she can't stop herself. Her maternal instincts didn't kick in for a second. (*Mirror*, 26 July 2008b)

These extracts highlight that similar to the case file material, despite the fact that both Alice and Chris lied to their sons, it was only Alice who was represented as a 'bad mother'. On the few occasions when Chris' bad parenting was referred to, it was always alongside Alice, thus he was represented as a 'bad parent' *with* Alice, rather than specifically a 'bad father' (for example, *The Times*, 7 December 2007; *Sunday Telegraph*, 9 December 2007). This implies that although being a 'bad mother' is viewed to be deviant behaviour, this notion is not extended to 'bad fathers', thus highlighting the gendered nature of this motif. This supports the theoretical perspective 'double deviancy', as Alice was judged not only for her role in the offending, but also due to her transgression against womanhood and particularly motherhood (Lloyd, 1995; Heidensohn, 1986).

Finally, while Janet Young was not directly constructed as a 'bad mother' in the same way as the previously discussed cases, this motif featured indirectly within the context of her wider representation as a 'scorned woman'. The notion of being or feeling 'scorned' is a gendered phenomenon, with phrases such as 'hell hath no fury like a woman scorned' being familiar expressions originating in Greek mythology and Renaissance literature (Simpson and Speake, 2009). Janet was constructed as a scorned woman, who wanted to take revenge on her husband following his affair and it was this that was represented as being a key motivator for her revealing the story of her taking his penalty points a number of years earlier. This is significant here, as

Janet's 'scorn' and revenge was blamed for the suggested damage that her role in the offending had upon her children, as evidenced by the following quotes:

You were motivated, I have no doubt, by an implacable desire for revenge, and with little consideration of the position of your wider family. (Judge's closing speech, 10 March 2013)

You engaged in a calculated course of conduct that was disastrous for your family. (Prosecution cross examination, 28 February 2013)

But how could a career woman as clever and accomplished as *Young* not realise the destruction of her family would almost certainly be a consequence of that? How could her obsessive hatred of *Crouch* blind her as to how her 'grand plan' to destroy him, might also destroy and humiliate her children? (*Daily Mirror*, 10 March 2013)

And here's where it got really horrid. Here's where she sacrificed her children in pursuit of her own defence. Long after this case is dead and buried in the law books, long after most of us have remembered how to spell *Crouch*, there will remain the stench of this sacrifice. (*Daily Mail*, 8 March 2013)

As highlighted by Jewkes (2015) the bad mother motif is so pervasive when constructing female offenders, that they are often described in this way irrespective of whether or not their offences involve children. The idealistic discourses surrounding motherhood played a key role in representing Janet as an antithesis of the 'good mother' narrative and consequently as a woman consumed by revenge. In addition, all five of Janet's children were over the age of 20 when the case went to trial (two of whom were over 30), therefore the use of language, such as 'children' and 'child' to describe them in the news media material is particularly noteworthy. By describing them in this way without identifying their ages, journalists were able to allude to their vulnerability and thus Janet's irresponsibility as a mother, irrespective of the fact that they were adults at the time of the offences and disclosure.

To summarise, the construction of Jane, Alice and Janet as 'bad mothers' was a key aspect of their wider representation as 'bad women'. As highlighted by Jacques and Radtke (2012: 444) 'disentangling ideals of womanhood from ideals of motherhood is virtually impossible', thus their representation as 'bad mothers' (albeit at differing levels), served to emphasise their deviancy both within and beyond the context of their offending.

'Sexual deviant'

It has been argued that sex is one of the most salient news values (Soothill and Walby, 1991; Greer, 2003; Jewkes, 2015), therefore the news media's preoccupation with particularly Jane and Sarah's supposed obsession with sex is hardly surprising when considered in this context. Benedict (1992) argues that there is a narrow range of typifications for female offenders, one of which being the 'virgin/whore' dichotomy. Heidensohn (1996) suggests that the 'fallen woman' narrative extends beyond sex-workers and female offenders whose criminality involves sex offences and it is frequently applied to most, if not all, female offenders, particularly those who commit typically unfeminine crimes, such as crimes against children.

Child sex offences are viewed to be 'crimes against morality' (Hayes and Baker, 2014) and are understood as being 'male crimes' both by the public and often within the academic community (Gavin, 2009). However, this articulation of the normative frame of masculinity as a way of understanding and explaining the sexual abuse of children also essentialises female child sex offenders within a normative frame of femininity and transforms their experiences into a masculine, objective version of the offence (Hayes and Baker, 2014). Considering this wider context of the construction of female child sex offending, Jane and her role in the co-offending were simplistically constructed as 'sexually deviant'. This particularly centred on the suggestion that she had an unhealthy obsession with sex, which eventually led her to have 'plumbed new depths of depravity' (judge's closing speech, 15 December 2009) by engaging in sex offences against children. It is significant to note that within the case file material, it was not Jane's obsession with sex that served to represent her as a bad woman, but rather her obsession with *depraved* sex, or more specifically, her supposed interest in having sex with children. This contradicts Jane's claim that she had 'no sexual interest in children' (Jane police interview, 20 June 2009), which shall be discussed further later. Furthermore, Jane's search for a more exciting sex life was described as her wanting 'a bit of spice' (Judge's closing speech, 15 December 2009; prosecution argument, November 2009) and when this quote is considered within the context of her criminality, this 'quest' was thus constructed as being both sinister yet superficial in equal measure. By constructing Jane as a sexually depraved woman, legal and media professionals were able to demonstrate the extent to which her sexual obsession deviated against the expectations of the idealised image of the virtuous and sexually pure 'Madonna', thus firmly defining her as the 'whore' antithesis (Benedict, 1992; Naffine, 1996).

Similar to the case file material, throughout the reporting of this case the news media constructed Jane as a woman who had always been obsessed with sex, but this eventually 'spiralled into sexual depravity' (*Daily Mail*, 5 November 2010). This depraved 'sex obsession' was the main aspect of Jane's character that was reported on in the news media and when quantified, the term 'sex' was mentioned in 363/476 articles about Jane and similarly to the case file material, this term was most frequently represented within the context of her child sexual abuse.

Furthermore, Jane's obsession with sex and specifically depraved sex was often explicitly linked to 'paedophilia' and the crimes that she had committed. By interchanging her obsession with sex and paedophilia in this way, journalists were able to construct Jane's interest in sex as an extension of her offences, thus rendering the two indistinguishable. For example, *The Daily Mail* (2 October 2009b) interchanged Jane's sexual interest and her search for 'excitement' with quotes such as 'police believe she was now hooked on the idea of having sexual contact with children', thus suggesting that her desire for new and 'exciting' sexual activities involved children.

By emphasising Jane's 'obsession' with sex, the news media were able to construct her as a 'bad' woman by linking her interest in sex with her engagement in taking indecent images of children. By constantly referring to Jane as a paedophile or a 'paedo' (for example, *Sun*, 16 December 2009c; *Daily Star*, 14 October 2009b; *Mirror*, 13 October 2009a) the news media is ascribing the various stereotypical images and connotations to Jane that this identity carries, such as monster, corrupters of innocent children and a corruptive force (Kincaid, 1998; Davidson, 2008; Hebenton and Seddon, 2009). Furthermore, as previously discussed, female child sex offenders are considered to be particularly morally corrupt, as they deviated against their gendered expectations as a woman and mother (Denov, 2004). Therefore, by representing Jane as inseparable from her child sex abuse crimes and her apparent 'sex obsession' in general, she is collectively constructed as a 'bad' woman and mother who is by her very nature and character, a paedophile.

Similar to the Jane Turner case, Sarah Johnson was constructed as a 'whore' within the 'virgin/whore dichotomy' (Benedict, 1992), particularly within the news media. Within the context of the case file material, Sarah was frequently questioned about her sex life during her police interviews. This is demonstrated by the following extracts and questions from police officers:

PO: How soon after you knew *David* did you have sex with him?
Sarah: Couple of days
PO: How regularly would you say…
Sarah: Quite regularly
PO: What would you call quite regularly? (*Sarah Johnson* police interview, 17 August 2002)

Police: who normally initiates sex between you?
Police: Do you watch or look at porn together?
Police: Do you ever talk about sex together?

Police: Do you and *David* share sexual fantasies?

Police: Have you ever shared sexual fantasies about children, *Sarah*? (Sarah responded 'No comment' to each question, Sarah Johnson, police interview, 18 August 2002)

Even when Sarah suggested that she had a 'much more emotional relationship with *David* rather than a physical one' (Sarah Johnson, police interview, 17 August 2002), she was still probed on the subject. The questioning on the subject became so excessive that her solicitor interjected with 'Haven't we explored this enough?' (Sarah Johnson, police interview, 17 August 2002). Although asking questions about the nature of Sarah's relationship with David would have been standard police procedure, the extent to which she was interrogated about their sex life and the explicit nature of the questions is particularly significant. David received similar questioning, however this is arguably expected, due to the potential sexual nature of his offences and his history of sexual violence (he had numerous previous sex offending charges, including having sex with a minor and rape, but he was never convicted) (David Fox, police interviews, 17 August 2002). However, Sarah was not being charged with crimes of a sexual nature or with the murder of the girls, yet her questioning on the subject of sex was not dissimilar to David's and the nature of the questions, particularly those which questioned her 'sexual fantasises' and whether or not she had a 'sexual interest in children', implied that she was potentially sexually deviant (Sarah Johnson, police interview, 17 August 2002). This therefore constructed her as a 'deviant' and 'fallen' woman, not only due to the nature of her offences, but also due to her implied 'perverse' sex life, regardless of the fact that she provided no comment to all such questioning.

Within the context of the news media material, Sarah's sex life was predominantly discussed in the tabloid newspapers and when mentioned in broadsheet articles, it was often in the form of direct quotes from the trial (for example, *Guardian*, 5 December 2003; *Independent*, 5 December 2003a). A potential explanation for this is that tabloid newspapers in particular often report on personal issues which serve to individualise and personalise crime actors (Jewkes, 2015). In tabloid newspapers in particular, Sarah's sex life and behaviour was described as extrovert and 'wild' (*Daily Star*, 19 August 2002), particularly on 'nights out'. For example, it was suggested that she loved to 'show off her bumblebee tattoo on her left breast' (*Daily Star*, 19 August 2002) and 'after a couple of drinks she would get up on the tables and start dancing and flashing her boobs' (*Daily Mail*, 20 August 2002). By following phrases such as this with descriptions of her sexual preferences and habits, the news media represented Sarah's supposed 'party lifestyle' and her sex life as being directly associated. Furthermore, one of the dominant narratives used within the context of this motif was that Sarah was obsessed by sex or 'sex mad'. This is evidenced by the following quotes:

> *Johnson* couldn't get enough sex – the raunchier and riskier the better. (*People*, 21 December 2003)

> She reinvented herself as a sex crazed vamp. (*Daily Mail*, 18 December 2003c)

> Partygoers said that she drank heavily and was hungry for sex. (*Sun*, 18 December 2003)

The extracts above echo the 'sex obsessed' discourses discussed in the Jane Turner case study, highlighting the cross-case relevance of this representation. The majority of the content of the tabloid articles related to Sarah's sex life consisted of extracts from various 'interviews' with Sarah's ex-partners. Although the news media used this as a tool to strengthen the claims made in the articles, the reliability of such sources can be questioned. Police statements were taken from a number of Sarah's ex-partners, many of which were used as 'sources' in the articles cited above, yet they were not used as witnesses during the trial, which questions their relevance to the overall case. This therefore suggests that while Sarah's sex life and supposed 'sex obsession' was not deemed to be significant for the trial itself, the news media constructed this as a significant aspect of Sarah's case, personality and lifestyle. This also highlights the journalistic tendency to place disproportionate attention to personal and individualised aspects of a criminal case, irrespective of their relevance to the trial and wider case proceedings (Jewkes, 2015; Nobles and Schiff, 2004).

In addition, it was also suggested in the tabloid reporting of this case that Sarah enjoyed 'wild', 'weird' and 'bizarre' sex (*People*, 25 August 2002). Such language implies that Sarah is 'depraved', which consequently represented her as a 'deviant woman' who wilfully defied her gender role expectations (Ballinger, 2000). This is evidenced by the following quotes:

> Weird sex, scratching, biting and stilettoes…our hell in bizarre world of *Sarah*. (*People*, 25 August 2002)

> In bed, she liked to keep her stilettoes on, and nothing else. She liked rough sex. (*Daily Mail*, 18 December 2003a)

> Randy raver *Sarah Johnson* howled so loudly during a sex romp in a conservatory horrified neighbours had to keep their kids indoors. (*Daily Star*, 18 December 2003)

The use of animalistic language to describe Sarah's sexual practices, such as 'scratching', 'rough' and 'wild', implied that her sex life was both depraved and abnormal, which served to construct Sarah as a 'fallen' woman and thus the antithesis of the idealised, virginal image of 'Madonna'. Furthermore, the sources of these assertions are somewhat questionable, as most were referred to as 'ex-boyfriends', 'neighbours' or simply as 'a source', within the article rather than being identified individuals directly involved in the case or trial. With this in mind, the relevance of many of the 'sources' listed above to the wider case proceedings is somewhat partial.

The potential reasons as to why Jane and Sarah were constructed as 'sexually deviant' are twofold. First, both cases received a high volume of media coverage and as sex is a key news value (Soothill and Walby,

1991), the emphasis on the women's sex obsession simultaneously represents them as 'fallen women', while reinforcing the human interest in the story. Second, both of the women's offending involved children, with Jane's being of a sexual nature. Offences against children are viewed to be among the most immoral, unnatural offending for a woman to engage in, therefore by representing the women as sexually deviant, they were represented as 'other' both within the context of their offending and their personal life.

Women co-offenders as 'others'

A key similarity between the way in which each of the women were portrayed, is that they were all represented in varying forms as 'others', who are distinctly different types of people, or more notably women, to the rest of society. 'Othering' is a process whereby certain individuals or groups are either directly or indirectly excluded from society, usually due to them being a perceived threat to the social order (Riggins, 1997; Ajzenstandt and Shapira, 2012).

A key aspect of this 'othering' process for the co-accused women was to construct them as 'non-human' by comparing them to or representing them as monsters, animals or mythical creatures. Janet was often described using animalistic and mythical language, for example, she was described as being 'savage' (*Daily Mail*, 8 March 2013), having a 'hunger for vengeance' (*Express*, 8 March 2013), a 'vindictive banshee' (*Sun*, 9 March 2013b) and was also compared to the mythical creature 'Medea' (*Mail on Sunday*, 10 February 2013). As highlighted by Jewkes (2015: 123), the images of women that still prevail in the media derive from 'pagan mythology, Juedo-Christian theology and classical art and literature'. Journalists often openly compared Janet to Greek mythological characters, such as Medea, who when neglected by her lover consequently murdered her children. By comparing Janet to Medea and other 'mythical monsters' in this way, patriarchal fears about female offenders become entangled with folk law myths about monsters and mythical creatures and characters, thus serving to firmly place her into the category of the 'other' (Jewkes, 2015).

In addition, although Chris (Alice's co-offender) was frequently compared to 'Reggie Perrin' (for example, *Daily Star*, 6 December 2007; *The Times*, 7 December 2007; *Daily Telegraph*, 8 December 2007b), a character from a British television comedy series who faked his own death, Alice was comparatively likened to the historical, manipulative female character of 'Lady Macbeth' (*Daily Mail*, 12 December 2007), who 'fulfilled almost all the requirements of a criminal woman imbued with evil' (Heidensohn, 1996: 91). This differential use of language highlights that while Chris' role in the offending was minimised and to some extent ridiculed, Alice's involvement in the fraudulent offences required the reference of a familiar motif of a manipulative and deceptive female character for the reader to make sense of her offending role. This highlights the ways in which men's offending is normalised, whereas women's offending, irrespective of its nature, is 'othered' and is often explained using over-simplistic and gendered narratives, which are rooted in mythical symbolism.

Furthermore, both Jane and Sarah were openly and indirectly compared to Myra Hindley, particularly in news media. Myra Hindley is in many ways the archetypal female (co)offender and it has been argued that her notoriety has yet to be eclipsed by any other female offender (Birch, 1993). Despite Hindley and her partner Ian Brady's crimes taking place in the 1960s, many serious female offenders continue to be compared to her. Jane was occasionally directly compared to Myra Hindley in news media, as evidenced by the extracts below:

> *Turner*, who has been compared to evil Moors murderer Myra Hindley. (*Daily Star*, 2 October 2009a)

> She is no better than Myra Hindley. (*People*, 4 October 2009)

> *Jane Turner* is right up there with Myra Hindley and Rose West in the malevolent club of vile and evil female monsters. (*Sun*, 3 October 2009b)

The last quotation mentioned above is particularly significant, as while Jane was openly compared to Myra Hindley and Rosemary West, both notorious female murderers, Simon (Jane's co-offender) was not compared to their male counterparts, Ian Brady and Fred West. This suggests that although notorious female offenders are needed as points of reference to the reader to demonstrate the depraved extent of Jane's crimes, due to the rarity of such offences, well-known male offenders are not required as a comparative tool to evidence Simon's depravity. This is arguably due to male child sex offending being perceived to be more common and therefore less shocking in comparison to the female counterpart (Hayes and Baker, 2014).

By making such comparisons between Jane and female offenders such as Myra Hindley, the reader is instantly directed to view Jane as being as evil as 'the most hated woman in Britain' (Birch, 1993; Murphy and Whitty, 2006). Furthermore, while Jane was only directly compared to Myra Hindley in ten articles, there are various indirect similarities between the reporting of Hindley and Turner, particularly when considering the use of language. For example, Myra Hindley was often referred to as being 'pure evil' and the 'personification of evil' (Birch, 1993) and similarly Jane's criminality was also often explained by her inherent 'evil' nature, for example, she was referred to as a 'woman of purest evil' (*Sun*, 16 December 2009c).

Comparisons to Hindley were more prevalent and direct in Sarah Johnson's case, potentially due to the notable similarities between the two women. For example, both women co-offended with their male partner, both argued that they were 'under their partner's spell' and both of their crimes involved children. Despite not committing a violent crime herself, Sarah experienced 'guilt through association, not just from *David Fox*, but from Myra herself' (Jones and Wardle, 2010: 62).

It is important to note that direct comparisons between Johnson and Hindley were predominantly evident in the tabloid material, rather than the broadsheet articles analysed. On the occasions when Hindley was mentioned in broadsheet articles, it was mainly to highlight that during Sarah's testimony, she had stated that fellow prison inmates had branded her 'Myra Hindley the second' (*The Times*, 5 December

2003). However, the differences between the tabloid and broadsheet reporting were mostly examples of differing methods of articulation and language use, rather than differing perspectives and ideologies.

Journalists used specific linguistic techniques to make the direct association between Hindley and Sarah Johnson. This is evidenced by the following extracts:

Sarah: Why I believe she's the new Myra. (*Daily Mail*, 19 December 2003b)

Like Ian Brady and Myra Hindley, the names *David Fox* and *Sarah Johnson* have become bywords for evil. (*Express*, 18 December 2003a)

Just as her police photo resembled Hindley's in the strong face marred by a surly stare and in the circumstances, obscene defiance, so there was something about her performance at the Old Bailey, a hardness between the self-obsession and self-pity, that raised uncomfortable echoes of the 1966 trial of Myra Hindley. (*Express*, 18 December 2003b)

By making the comparisons highlighted above, the news media firmly constructed Sarah as a 'deviant woman' not only due to the crimes that she committed, but also due to her associations and similarities with Myra Hindley. The comparisons with Hindley, who remains to be the archetypal 'deviant' and 'monstrous' woman, enabled journalists to make a clear distinction between 'us' and 'them', thus exemplifying Young's (1999) concept of the 'manufacture of monsters'. Young (1999) argues that the mass media plays a key role in the othering and demonisation process of offenders, therefore Sarah's indirect affiliation with Hindley and direct association with David ensured that she was constructed as 'other' and a bad woman.

Young (1999: 104) argues essentialism is vitally important when creating 'others', as 'it separates out human groups on the basis of their culture or nature'. With this in mind, although it could be argued that all offenders, particularly those who engage in serious criminality, are viewed to be 'others', in the current research, the women were more readily given this label in comparison to their male partners irrespective of their level of criminality and/or involvement. This could arguably be due to the perceived rarity and abnormality of female offending and the consequential lack of a simple and familiar explanation for such behaviour. By routinely representing female (co)offenders within this 'other' motif, journalists in particular are failing to offer an adequate and satisfactory explanation for the women's offending behaviour, thus questioning journalistic practice when reporting on this issue.

In summary, in both the case file and news media material, each of the women were represented according to the discourses surrounding appropriate femininity (Smart, 1976; Heidensohn, 1996; Ballinger, 2000). Within the news media material, various journalistic practices, such as selection, exclusion, elaboration and the use of stereotypical images and metaphors (Entman, 1993; Tankard, 2001), were used to construct the women in gendered and essentialist ways, which were often based on stereotypical assumptions surrounding female offending. Similar to previous research exploring female offending (Jewkes, 2015; Naylor, 2001; Wykes, 1998), the representation of the female co-offenders in this research suggests that journalists have a stock number of narratives for female offenders, which they use, often interchangeably, as strategies of guilt or blame in order for the reader to attempt to make sense of 'deviant' women. In the current research, a number of motifs and narratives emerged which support existing research, such as 'bad mother' (Jewkes, 2015; Barnett, 2006) and sexually deviant (Jewkes, 2015; Heidensohn, 1996; Edwards, 1984). However, by positioning the women within gendered narratives, their voices, stories and perspectives were consequently silenced and reinterpreted to fit within existing stock motifs of female offending (Barlow, 2015). Journalists in particular emphasised the 'otherness' of the women by focusing on the deviant nature of their offending as *women,* which led to their versions of events and reasons for offending to not be fully considered.

Equally bad or worse? The representation of women-co-offenders offending role

In order to gain a more holistic understanding of the social construction of the co-accused women, the representation of their offending role and participation in their criminality needs to be critically analysed. As previously discussed, the social construction of female co-offending/offenders has received minimal scholarly attention. However, existing research suggests that women in co-offending partnerships tend to be represented more harshly in comparison to male counterparts (Grabe et al, 2006; Skilbrei, 2013; Jewkes, 2015). In all of the cases analysed, each of the women were constructed to be more or at least equally to blame in comparison to their male co-offender, irrespective of their level of criminal involvement.

Jane was predominantly represented as the 'main offender', despite there being four other co-offenders involved in the offences, all of whom were convicted and received lengthy prison sentences. One aspect of this began in the initial stages of the reporting and centres on the fact that Jane was the main focus of the vast majority of news articles. On the day that Jane was charged, despite Simon being charged the previous day, she was the focus of every headline relating to the case during this time period. This highlights that from the early stages of the case, the intention was to construct Jane as the main offender, thus minimising the role and involvement of other members of the offending group. By focusing the attention on Jane in the initial stages of reporting, the reader is encouraged to not only see her as the 'main offender', but to rather see her as the 'only' offender, thus representing her as a solo rather than a co-offender.

Furthermore, when this was quantified, while Jane was mentioned in 476 articles, her co-offenders were mentioned by name to a much lesser extent, namely Simon 95 mentions (75 articles also mentioned Jane), Susan 55 mentions (52 also mentioned Jane), Louise 27 mentions (22 also mentioned Jane) and Tracey 26 mentions (nine also mentioned Jane). This demonstrates that not only was Jane directly referenced to a much greater extent than her co-defendants, but they were most frequently mentioned alongside her, thus consistently constructing her as the 'main offender.'

This focus on Jane remained consistent throughout the period of reporting analysed and her co-offenders were usually only mentioned towards the end of the article. For example, *The Sun* (16 December 2009c) article discussed the sentences given to Susan and Jane, yet Susan was only mentioned in the final paragraph and the remainder of the article talked about the 'depraved' and 'wicked' nature of Jane. This demonstrates that despite Susan and Jane both being charged and sentenced for child sex offences and irrespective of them both being part of the same offending network, Jane was constructed as the most culpable of the two. A potential explanation for this could be that while Susan was a former 'prostitute' (*Daily Mail*, 16 December 2009e; *Daily Telegraph*, 2 October 2009) who 'was living in abject' 'dirty' conditions in a 'council house' (*Guardian*, 2 October 2009), Jane was believed to be a 'bubbly and friendly person' (*The Times*, 2 October 2009a) who had a well-kept home and respectable family. Therefore, the portrayal of Susan's lifestyle as being 'deviant' before the offending served to represent Jane as being the most depraved and responsible out of the two, thus serving to over-emphasise Jane's culpability. Furthermore, a similar interpretation is that Jane's participation in the offences was represented as being more inexplicable and deviant due to her criminality leading to the breakdown of an example of the 'idealised' institution of the nuclear family.

Collectively, the overwhelming focus on Jane's participation in the offending is arguably due to her not only being woman and a mother engaging in child-sex offending, similar to the other women involved in the offending network, but she was also a nursery worker, thus making her gendered deviancy threefold. Furthermore, she didn't have the same 'deviant' and 'troubled' upbringing as the other women involved in the offending group, therefore there was less of a rational and plausible explanation available for her offending.

In addition, as well as being portrayed as the 'main offender', the news media often took this further and constructed Jane as the central, organising figure of the offending network, particularly in the stages of reporting prior to the trial. This is shown in the headlines and extracts below:

The ring was headed by *Turner* (*Mirror*, 19 October 2009b)

Pervert *Turner's* paedophile ring (*Daily Star*, 14 October 2009b)

Woman at centre of paedophile ring refuses to name her toddler victims. (*Daily Mail*, 2 October 2009b)

Tankard (2001) suggests that emphasising and elaborating on certain aspects of a case serves to represent a story in a particular way and for a particular purpose. By constructing Jane as the central figure, the news media is not only portraying her to be the most culpable co-offender, but is also simultaneously suggesting that she initiated, organised and controlled the offending network. This is despite the fact that she had never actually spoken to or heard of two of the co-offenders before her arrest and she had only communicated with Susan via the internet on two occasions. This particular journalistic technique was mostly evident during periods of reporting where Jane was particularly demonised, for example, when she refused to name her child victims and following the release of her police interview tapes by the CPS. By interchanging Jane as the 'main offender and as the 'central, organising figure' of the offending network, journalists were able to simultaneously exaggerate Jane's offences while minimising the involvement of her co-offenders, thus constructing her criminality as the most newsworthy and incomprehensible.

Similarly, Sarah was constructed to be as bad, if not worse, than David and in many instances she was represented as being his accomplice, despite being found not guilty of assisting an offender. Despite Sarah's crime being essentially providing an alibi for her partner, her involvement elicited a far stronger mediated public reaction than a charge of perverting the course of justice would usually merit (Jewkes, 2015: 143). From the beginning of the reporting of this case, following David and Sarah's initial questioning by police officers, it was frequently implied that Sarah had been charged with murder, as evidenced by headlines such as 'Couple charged over girls' murder' (*The Times*, 21 August 2002) and 'Troubled lives of couple suspected of murdering *Lucy* and *Katie*' (*Daily Telegraph*, 20 August 2002). Although the couple were initially held on suspicion of murder, it was only David who was eventually charged with the murder of Lucy and Katie. However, the above extracts highlight that Sarah was initially constructed as being an equal accomplice to David, thus exaggerating her role in the offending.

A further example of Sarah being constructed to be equally guilty to David centred upon the notion that she was often indirectly blamed for the deaths of Lucy and Katie. This was evidenced in two key ways. First, Sarah was blamed for triggering David's anger and the news media concluded that this led him to murder Lucy and Katie. It was suggested that following a phone call conversation with Sarah in the early evening of 4 August 2002 (the night the girls were murdered), David became very angry as he didn't want Sarah to go out with her mother. For example, it was suggested that 'Detectives believe that she put him in the state of mind to kill' (*Daily Star*, 18 December 2003). This highlights that despite Sarah not being in the area on the night that David murdered the children, the news media alluded to her involvement by blaming her for his anger. The second example of indirect blame towards Sarah emerged following the revelation that she had been spotted kissing another man on the night that David murdered Lucy and Katie. This is evidenced by the following quotes:

This is the sickening moment that sex-mad *Sarah Johnson* cheated on lover *David Fox* as he killed young school girls *Lucy* and *Katie*. (*Daily Star*, 18 December 2003)

Here is *Sarah Johnson* snogging a man on a wild night out – the same evening that *David Fox* killed *Lucy* and *Katie*. (*Sun*, 18 December 2003)

Sarah Johnson told police she was in the bath the night *Lucy* and *Katie* died. This is what she was really doing. (*Daily Mail*, 18 December 2003c)

Each of the above extracts were accompanied by an image of Sarah kissing a man (who was not David), which was placed directly underneath or next to the main headline. The tabloids in particular combined the image with headlines such as 'He killed while she was kissing' (*Daily Star*, 18 December 2003) and 'Kiss of death' (*Sun*, 18 December 2003), which again served to implicate Sarah as being indirectly guilty for the girl's murder. Overall, the news media in particular constructed Sarah as being 'equally bad and equally guilty' to David irrespective of their unequal involvement. The media portrayed David as a man capable of extreme cruelty, but without the actions of 'submissive' Sarah, he would not have been able to attempt to get away with his crimes.

Furthermore, there was also a similar emphasis on Alice's role in the offending and a minimisation of Chris' role in the Alice Jones case study. It is significant to note here that it was only Alice who faced a full trial for her involvement in the offending, as Chris pleaded guilty to all offences. This meant that within the context of the trial, the focus was disproportionately on Alice, which thus served to construct her as the most culpable offender. Despite Chris himself arguing that 'the plan was my idea. I gave her no choice but to go along with it' (Chris Jones, police interview, 6 December 2007) and that 'I was the one pulling the strings' (Chris Jones, police interview, 6 December, 2007), Alice was irrespectively constructed as the most culpable offender.

Upon initial analysis, it appeared that Chris may have been the focus of the news media reporting to a greater extent than Alice, as while the search term '*Chris Jones*' produced 500 articles during the time period analysed, '*Alice Jones*' produced 430 articles. However, when analysed further, most of the articles were the same for both search terms and significantly, 375/430 articles focused predominantly on Alice, 36/430 discussed both Alice and Chris, with an emphasis on the former and just 19 articles mentioned both Chris and Alice equally (this analysis was determined by which offender featured more prominently in both the headline and main body of the article).

Furthermore, most of the additional articles relating specifically to Chris featured during the initial four days of reporting and following the guilty verdict and there were significant lapses in reporting about Chris, particularly during the trial. However, the focus of reporting was consistently on Alice throughout the time period analysed. In spite of this, it is important to note that while a number of articles provided a balanced overview of the case and predominantly used a non-sensationalist reporting style (for example, *Guardian*, 6 December 2007) and a small number of articles, particularly opinion pieces, even portrayed Alice somewhat sympathetically (for example, *Mirror*, 10 December 2007b), on the whole, the portrayal of Alice was predominantly negative. This disproportionate and negative focus on Alice meant that her involvement in the offences was often exaggerated and viewed to be much more serious and significant in comparison to Chris' offending. There are a number of possible explanations for this harsher media treatment. For example, because she was a woman and serious female criminality is viewed as being more 'deviant' and a double transgression when compared to male criminality (Lloyd, 1995; Ballinger, 2000); or because she was found to have lied at various points during the case and therefore it was assumed that she was consequently lying about her innocence.

In addition, journalists frequently used distinctly different language to describe Alice and Chris, often within the same news articles:

Chris is an exemplary father figure who is now a broken man. He has been bullied in the 233 days he has so far spent in police custody and is taking medication for depression. (*The Times*, 24 July 2008 – quote from defence barrister)

She is a compulsive liar and her behaviour towards her children is despicable. (Quote from police officer)

'The family man who faked his own death'/'heartless *Alice*, who hoodwinked her sons'. (*Independent on Sunday*, 9 December 2007)

This differential language served to perpetuate the narrative that not only was Alice more to blame than Chris, but she was potentially more deviant and a societal concern. As highlighted by Heidensohn (1996) organised crime and fraud is more readily associated with male offending, therefore Alice's involvement in the fraudulent offences was more of a difficult concept for news media professionals to explain. This lack of understanding led to her involvement and role in the offending to be reduced to over-simplistic and gendered, stereotypical narratives, which are typically used to define female deviancy. This supports previous research, which argues that within male and female offending partnerships, particularly those involving violent offences, the female offender is more likely to receive negative and disproportionate media coverage in comparison to the male counterpart (Grabe et al, 2006; Jewkes, 2015). However, this case study suggests that this notion could also be extended to non-violent offences.

Furthermore, as previously mentioned, a key consequence of constructing Janet as a scorned, vengeful woman is that not only was she blamed for her role in the offences, but Janet and her desire for revenge was also inadvertently blamed for a number of issues external to the offending, notably for ruining Edward's career and negatively affecting the wellbeing and welfare of her children, as previously discussed. The notion of Janet being blamed for ruining Edward's career was particularly evident in the news media material, as highlighted below:

Ms *Young*, 60, then embarked on a vengeful campaign to bring *Crouch* down, jurors heard. (*The Times*, 6 February 2013a)

Furious *Janet Young* hoped to inflict 'maximum and probably fatal damage' to the politician's high-flying career, the court was told. (*Sun*, 6 February 2013a)

It was *Crouch's* decision one month later to walk out. It was *Young's* vengeful response thereafter that would lay waste everything they had worked together for. (*Guardian*, 8 March 2013)

However, while Janet's disclosure of the point swapping offence did undoubtedly have an impact on the 'downfall' of Edward's career, there was very little accountability placed on Crouch for his role in the offending and the potential impact that his actions had upon Janet's career, particularly in the press. Janet suggested that she had to make 'many sacrifices' (Janet, trial transcript, 26 February) for Crouch and his career. Although Janet had an established and successful career as an economist, she stated that 'I had to make certain career decisions to benefit my husband and family' (Janet Young, testimony, 26 February 2013), however Edward did not share these same responsibilities, due to the gendered nature of family and private sphere duties (Bernard, 1981). However, due to Edward's career 'downfall' fitting with the prescribed 'scorned woman' narrative and Janet's supposed all-encompassing desire for revenge, this was the dominant focus of the press reporting within this context. By alluding to a number of consequences of Janet's 'scorned' behaviour external to the offending, including the aforementioned implied impact on her children, legal professionals and journalists were able to exaggerate the impact of her revenge, while minimising the role of her co-offender, Edward Crouch.

The disproportionate blame placed on each of the women could be due to a combination of the media's fascination with female and male co-offenders (Jewkes, 2015), along with the women's perceived transgressions against their expected gender roles, as male offending is not viewed to be a societal threat or as newsworthy as women's offending due to its perceived normality (Ballinger, 2000; Lloyd, 1995). The media's solution to the problem of women who are equal partners, or at least, appear to go along unquestioningly with their male partner's wishes to commit criminal offences, 'is to place the burden of guilt on their shoulders' (Jewkes, 2015: 143). Although the male co-offenders were also demonised, their masculinity was not questioned, whereas the perceived compromise of the women's femininity was the focus of both legal and news media discourse. This supports existing literature, which argues that criminality is generally constructed as a masculine act (Naffine, 1987; Ballinger, 2000; Jewkes, 2011), therefore men's offending is normalised to a greater extent than women's criminality, irrespective of whether they commit crime together or individually.

Conclusion

Overall, the construction and representation of the co-accused women in legal and media discourse highlights that their explanations for offending, experiences and perspectives were not fully acknowledged. They were mostly constructed using familiar gendered motifs, such as sexual deviant (Jewkes, 2015; Heidensohn, 1996), bad mother (Barnett, 2006) and 'other' (Jewkes, 2015), all of which served to emphasise their double deviancy and transgressions from idealised versions of femininity and womanhood. Furthermore, their role in the offending was often exaggerated or emphasised, thus constructing them as 'equally bad' if not worse than their male counterparts, irrespective of their level of involvement. However, by constructing female co-offenders in this way, journalists in particular and legal professionals are failing to offer an adequate and nuanced explanation for such women's reasons for offending. The following chapter will consider an alternative, feminist approach to understanding potentially coerced women's reasons for offending.

FIVE
APPLYING THE 'CONTINUUM OF COERCION': AN ALTERNATIVE, FEMINIST FRAMEWORK

Introduction

This chapter begins by critiquing the representation of the women's reasons for offending as being a 'rational choice'. Furthermore, the chapter introduces an alternative feminist conceptual framework to gain a more nuanced understanding of coercion as a pathway into crime for co-offending women. This framework is applied to the case studies analysed in this research by drawing on the women's testimonies and experiences, taken from the case file material. The framework of a 'continuum of coercion' highlights the ways in which abusive, controlling and/or obsessive relationships with a male partner may influence a woman's 'decision' to offend and suggests that in some instances, such behaviours should be understood as being part of the wider continuum of domestic violence.

A rational choice?

A key similarly in the construction of the co-accused women is that the influence and impact of the personal relationship between the co-offenders was minimised in each of the cases. Jane's relationship with Simon was represented as being a 'wicked obsession' and was diminished due to their communication being restricted to an online relationship. The abuse and control that Sarah allegedly experienced in her relationship with David was not acknowledged as a potential influencing factor on her offending in the news media material in particular. Furthermore, the impact of Alice and Janet's controlling relationships were also rarely acknowledged in news media discourse. Rather than attempting to understand the nature of the relationship between the co-offenders, both journalists and legal professionals resorted to over-simplistic narratives, which were mostly defined by concepts such as 'rationality' and 'choice' to explain the women's reasons for offending. This consequently restricted the women's explanations to familiar motifs, which reflect hegemonic white, middle-class male experiences and reasons for offending (Ballinger, 2012).

A key aspect of this over-simplification of the co-accused women's perspectives centred on the notion that their reasons for offending were often limited to their decision being a 'rational choice'. A selection of evidential quotes from the case file material of each of the cases, which were also utilised in news media reports, have been outlined below:

JANE: 'This was not an isolated incident committed on the spur of the moment. This was wicked, cold, rational, calculated, repeated offending, which for any decent person defies belief. You made the choice.' (Judge's closing speech, December, 2009, extracts cited in *The Mirror*, 16 December 2009d; *The Times*, 16 December 2009b)

ALICE: 'Despite your efforts to put all the blame on your husband with your defence of marital coercion, I am convinced that you played your part in the fraud efficiently and wholeheartedly.' (Judge's closing speech, 24 July 2008, extracts cited in *The Mirror*, 24 July 2008)

SARAH: 'You had plenty of opportunity to refuse to persist in a course of lying and deception, you chose not to.' (Judge's closing speech, 17 December 2003, cited in *The Independent*, 18 December 2003b)

JANET: 'She plays an important role in the running of our country, yet she was unable to reject the suggestions of her husband? She did something because she chose to do it.' (Prosecution opening speech, 12 February 2013, extracts cited in *The Times*, 6 February 2013b)

This emphasis on rational choice in each of the cases highlights that legal professionals, particularly the prosecution and the judge, as well as print media journalists failed to understand the context in which the women's 'choices' were made. However, each of the women's explanations for their offending did not fit with this concept of 'rational choice', as outlined below:

JANE: 'I wanted to make him happy. At the time I would have done anything to make him happy. Looking back at the situation, I'm fuming with myself really – I am because it's like the epitome isn't it, it's like absolutely disgusting and I know, you know, it's just awful.' (Jane Turner, police interview, 19 June 2009)

SARAH: 'I lied to protect him. I loved him very much.' (Sarah Johnson, testimony, 5 and 6 December 2003)

ALICE: 'He knew how to make me feel insignificant. He made me feel like I didn't really count. All the major decisions were made by him. Whatever he wanted to do, I did.' (Alice Jones, testimony, 17 July 2008)

JANET: 'It didn't look to me like I had a choice at all in the matter, so I took the form and signed it. I had been worn down over a long period of time and it looked to me like it was the only thing I could do to get him off my case and keep my marriage together.' (Janet Young, testimony, 25 February 2013)

Furthermore, both Alice and Janet cited the defence of 'marital coercion' during their trials (the defence was abolished in the UK in 2014), thus highlighting the suggested significance and influence of their husband's coercive behaviour on their reasons for offending. Both women suggested that it was their husband's control and emotional abuse, which led them to be coerced into crime. Janet argued that she felt 'pushed into a corner' and 'worn down by (*Edward's*) constant pressure and control' (Janet Young, testimony, 26 February 2013), while Alice argued that Chris was 'manipulative' and 'had a habit of making (her) feel quite small and inadequate' (Alice, testimony, 17 July 2008). However, this was openly questioned and ridiculed by journalists and legal professionals in two key ways. First, the defence itself was openly questioned, particularly in the Janet Young case. For example, it was referred to as a 'defence from the middle ages' (*The Times*, 8 March 2013c) that to 'all modern sensibilities is absurd' (prosecution summary, 4 March 2013). There are a number of issues with the defence of marital coercion, such as a woman had to be married to cite the defence, the husband had to be present at the time of the offence, thus contradicting research which suggests that coercive control can occur without the physical presence of the controller (Stark, 2007; Welle and Falkin, 2000) and it could be argued that the defence denies women agency. However, as argued by Yeo (1993), the majority of legal defences have been developed on the basis of male experiences and despite defences such as marital coercion having a number of issues, developing defences specifically for women at least attempts to account for the differences between men and women's experiences of offending and criminality.

Furthermore, by focusing on the notion that the defence is a 'legal relic of the middle ages' (*The Times*, 8 March 2013c) and on the implied lack of applicability to the twenty-first century, both journalists and, unsurprisingly, the prosecution placed emphasis on the weakness of the defence itself rather than focusing on the women's perspective and explanations for their involvement in the offending. In addition, this ridicule led to a lack of acknowledgement that this was the only defence available which at least attempted to account for women who suggest that they have been coerced into crime by a male partner. For example, while the defence of duress concerns defendants who have been threatened with death or serious injury to commit the offences for which they were charged, this fails to account for non-physical threats to which women can often be subject, such as psychological pressures and moral threats (Yeo, 1993). With all of this in mind, it is argued here that the criticisms of the defence of marital coercion should not have been used as a reason to minimise the potential influence that Edward and Chris' controlling behaviour had upon Janet and Alice's reasons for offending. Although it is unsurprising that the prosecution adopted this perspective, journalists could have attempted to provide a more balanced overview of the women's reasons for citing the defence, rather than ridiculing the defence itself.

Furthermore, for both women, there was an overwhelming emphasis on the 'type' of woman they were perceived to be and the potential influence that this may have had on their capacity to be coerced. Examples are cited below:

> She is a woman who has spent her life making important decisions and choices. She is a very influential woman who has had a glittering career as an economist, she is a visiting lecturer at a number of universities, she has been a chief economic advisor, she earns a six-figure sum and has run for the equal right to choose. Do you really think that she would do something because some man told her to? (Janet Young, prosecution opening speech, 25 February 2013)

> You played an equal role in this offence, you are not a victim. (Alice Jones, prosecution statement, 15 July 2008)

> PO: *Alice*, you're an adult.
> *Alice:* I know.

PO: You're an intelligent woman and you had a choice, didn't you?

Alice: No, I don't feel like I did. (Alice Jones, police interview, 10 December 2007)

Can a gifted woman who advises on the affairs of nations become so subjugated in a marriage that she has no freedom of choice? (Janet Young, *Sunday Times*, 10 February 2013)

However, by implying that only certain 'types' of women are able to be coerced, there was a failure to adequately understand the nature of abusive relationships. Weitzman (2000) suggested that society is less willing to accept that upper class, educated or privileged women experience abuse, domestic violence and/or control and that even abused, privileged women themselves do not recognise domestic abuse in their own relationships due to their internalisation of stereotypes about abused women. Furthermore, Berg (2014) suggests that privileged women who have influential careers and are thus seen to be in control of various aspects of their environment are likely to blame themselves if they are unable to control and sustain their marriage. With this in mind, irrespective of Janet or Alice's education or class status, this does not render them incapable of being coerced or exempt them from being in a potentially abusive, violent or controlling relationship.

Overall, in spite of Alice and Janet's suggestions that their partners had controlled them throughout their marriage and that this had influenced their decision to offend, the legal and media discourse focused on the issues with the defence of marital coercion itself and implied that both Alice and Janet were not the 'type' of women who were able to be coerced, which consequently served to minimise and discredit their experiences and perspectives (Barlow, 2015b).

With all of this in mind, the perspectives offered by each of the women did not fit with the male defined version of rationality or rational choice, therefore their version of events were not fully acknowledged in both court and the print media. While each of the women placed great significance on the influence of their relationship with their male partner on their reasons for offending, such explanations were redefined to fit with the male defined epistemology which characterises legal thought (Yeo, 1993; Ballinger, 2012). However, as highlighted by Ballinger (2012: 452), 'to make assumptions about the population as a whole based on such constructions is to privilege the understanding of the world of the group which has dominated legal and public life: white, middle-class, heterosexual men'. This legal and public domination of the male perspective has led to all experiences and behaviour which falls outside these parameters to be 'othered' and consequently silenced or muted (Barlow, 2015b; Ballinger, 2012; Carline, 2005). Ballinger (2012: 452) argues that such principles lead to a double exclusion of the female experience, due to both the gendered nature of the law and male knowledge being viewed to be hierarchically more valuable.

'Continuum of coercion'

With this in mind, rather than limiting women co-offenders' reasons for offending to over-simplistic binaries or explanations, this research utilises and applies Stark's (2007) coercive control theory and Kelly's (1988) 'continuum of sexual violence' to develop a new conceptual framework, 'a continuum of coercion'. This attempts to explain co-offending women's pathways into crime by utilising the women's own accounts and perspectives on their relationship and offending. This notion of a coercive pathway into crime combines Stark's (2007: 78) definition of 'coercive control', namely, 'calculated, malevolent conduct deployed almost exclusively by men to dominate individual women by intervening repeated physical abuse with three equally important tactics, namely intimidation, isolation and control' with Kelly's (1988) notion of a 'sexual continuum'. Kelly (1988) argues that the continuum of sexual violence ranges from extensions of the myriad forms of sexism women encounter every day through to rape or murder of women by men. She suggests that the concept of a continuum enables women to make sense of their experiences by showing how 'typical' and 'extreme' male behaviours shade into one another. Although Kelly (1988) and Stark's (2007) ideas concern domestic and sexual abuse, their concepts can be reapplied to explain the 'continuum of coercion' with relation to committing crimes. It is argued here that rather than limiting the women's reasons for offending to simplistic, gendered explanations, which leads to the silencing, muting or distorting of their perspectives, the notion of a 'continuum of coercion' could better explain the women's pathways into crime.

This concept argues that a range of behaviours could be considered as being potentially coercive within male and female co-offending partnerships, particularly those that are characterised by a personal relationship. The definition of 'coercion' is the 'action or practice of persuading someone to do something by using force or threats' (Oxford English Dictionary, 2015). The legal definition of coercion, such as that cited in the defence of marital coercion, often emphasises physical force or threat as being the main, if not only, possibly coercive technique. However increasingly, other methods, such as coercive control, psychological abuse and non-physical threats are being recognised as potentially coercive behaviours (Welle and Falkin, 2000; Jones, 2008). With this in mind, when referring to coercion within the context of the 'continuum of coercion' discussed here, the concept is defined as the action or practice of persuading, forcing or encouraging someone to do something by using force, threats, abuse (including physical, psychological, economic and/or emotional), manipulation (including love or obsession) and/or control. Furthermore, rather than being viewed as distinct and separate forms of coercive behaviour, the often over-lapping nature of such coercive techniques is acknowledged within this conceptual framework. As evidenced in the case studies analysed here, many coercive behaviours are present in the same relationship, therefore categorising and separating such experiences does not accurately reflect the reality of many coerced women's lives. In addition, this conceptual framework suggests that within the context of such co-offending partnerships, the whole relationship should be explored when attempting to understand the women's reasons for offending, rather than focusing exclusively on the offending act itself. This leads to a more nuanced understanding of what factors and behaviours may lead to some women being coerced into crime in the first place, such as their relationship with their male partner/co-offender (among other possible explanations and mitigating factors), rather than viewing their offending in isolation.

Each of the women alluded to such coercive techniques during their police interviews, witness statements and court testimonies. For example, although Jane was not physically forced into crime by Simon, her police interviews and key defence arguments suggest that she was emotionally coerced or at least significantly influenced by him. This case study highlights the significance of viewing a range of behaviours as potentially coercive, beyond the scope of physical force, as Jane argued that the influence of her relationship with Simon and her 'infatuation' with him played a significant role in her reasons for offending. Jane argued that she 'loved' Simon and would have 'done anything to make him happy' (Jane Turner, police interviews and witness statement, June 2009). She suggested that Simon encouraged her to view the exchange of indecent imagery of children as an integral aspect of their relationship and consequently a way to make him happy. The notion of viewing child sex offences as a significant aspect of a relationship is a familiar technique used by male child sex offenders who co-offend with women (Matthews et al, 1991). However, although Simon suggested to Jane that he also had emotional feelings towards her, following his arrest he admitted that he had never had such feelings, thus implying that he used her 'obsession' with him to obtain the indecent imagery of children for his own gain. In addition, Jane's case adds a complex third dimension to the 'continuum of coercion', as Jane and Simon's relationship was restricted to online rather than face-to-face communication. However, relationships online can intensify much quicker than 'real world' relationships and strong emotional bonds can develop quickly (Dombrowski et al, 2007; Henry-Waring and Barraket, 2008). With this in mind, the fact that Jane and Simon had never met in person may not completely minimise the potential coercive impact of their relationship on Jane's offending.

Sarah's case is arguably the most typical example of a coercive relationship out of the four case studies analysed. This case highlights the relevance of viewing coercion into crime as a continuum, as it encompasses various aspects of the coercive behaviour mentioned previously. For example, Sarah argued that throughout her relationship with David he was both emotionally and physically abusive and that 'no-one had any idea what sort of relationship (she) had with that man' (Sarah, court testimony, 5 and 6 December 2003). She suggested that he controlled various aspects of her life, for example, he prevented her from seeing friends and family and wanted her to leave her job as a teaching assistant, despite this making her happy (Sarah Johnson, case file, accessed March 2013). However, Sarah attempted to rationalise this control during her police interviews in particular by suggesting that David was 'the old fashioned sort' and 'that's just the way he's been brought up' (Sarah Johnson, police interview, 17 August 2002). This highlights the ways in which the patriarchal expectations of womanhood and femininity, namely being passive and a submissive partner, allowed Sarah to rationalise David's behaviour and expectations. Furthermore, Sarah provided examples of physical abuse during her relationship, such as being kicked and slapped by David (Sarah Johnson, police interview, 17 August 2002). A particular example is cited below:

> *Sarah:* I can't really remember what the argument was about, but he just slapped me across the face and because of my bone structure it bruised, but it wasn't like a fist in my face or anything, it was just like a sort of slap sort of thing, to shut me up really.
>
> *PO:* And how did you react?
>
> *Sarah:* Shocked, it shut me up and he was very sorry about it, he just couldn't stand me banging on.
>
> *PO:* When you say he couldn't stand you banging on, do you feel that you deserved the slap that you got then?
>
> *Sarah:* I can't answer that question, at the time I know, well, I can understand the other side of it as well.

PO: So did you accept his behaviour?

Sarah: Yeah. (Sarah Johnson, police interview, 17 August 2002).

The above exchange suggests that Sarah accepted David's physical abuse, as she minimised his behaviour by arguing that it was her fault. Research suggests that this is a common deflective tactic that victims of domestic violence use to rationalise, minimise and excuse their partner's violent behaviour (Wood, 2001; Eckstein, 2011). Furthermore, despite Sarah initially suggesting that David had only hit her on one occasion, described in the above exchange, later in the interview she revealed that he had 'kicked me before' in an argument and that 'apart from that just normal pushing' (Sarah Johnson, police interview, 17 August 2002). This suggests that although Sarah recognised that David had been violent towards her during their relationship, she accepted his behaviour because she blamed herself for provoking it. This highlights the importance of exploring the whole relationship when attempting to understand coercion as a pathway into crime, as controlling and violent behaviour is often minimised by the male partner/co-offender and becomes a normalised aspect of the relationship (Stark, 2007; Welle and Falkin, 2000).

With regard to Sarah's role in the co-offending, Sarah and her defence team suggested a number of key reasons as to why she provided the false alibi for David on the night of Lucy and Katie's murder. The main reason provided was that she lied to protect David and Sarah used this explanation in both her police interviews and trial testimony. She stated in both contexts that she lied to 'protect him' as he had 'been accused of attacking a girl' in the past, which caused him to have a 'nervous breakdown' and she 'couldn't see him go through that again' (Sarah Johnson, police interview, 17 August 2002). During her police interviews, Sarah argued that she believed David to be incapable of murder, as she stated that 'I know him inside out, he's a very emotional person, he wouldn't be capable of doing that' (Sarah Johnson, police interview, 17 August 2002). During her trial testimony, Sarah also argued that she had 'no idea' that David had murdered the girls and that she 'lied to protect the man (she) loved very much' (Sarah Johnson, testimony, 3 and 4 December 2003). Sarah's explanations that she lied to protect David because she loved him are supported by previous research, as Jones (2008) argued that women often commit crime on behalf of and/or with their partner out of love.

An additional explanation that Sarah and her defence team offered for her providing the alibi for David is that Sarah felt 'pushed into a corner' to lie for him (Sarah Johnson, testimony, 3 and 4 December 2003). For example, she stated that 'I was scared. I was going home to that man at the end of the day, it's very embarrassing to be in a relationship like that' (Sarah Johnson, testimony, 3 and 4 December 2003). This highlights that in such instances of co-offending, all aspects of the offender's relationship need to be explored to gain a broader understanding of how this may have an impact upon the offending behaviour. Previous research suggests that fear is a strong motivator in women's co-offending (Richie, 1996; Welle and Falkin, 2000; Jones, 2008), as is committing an offence out of love for one's partner (Jones, 2008; Jones, 2011). Sarah argued that she provided the false alibi for David both out of fear and love for him. It is therefore argued here that love and fear should not be viewed as two distinct pathways into crime, but that such experiences should be understood as part of a continuum of coercion into crime.

Both Alice and Janet cited the defence of 'marital coercion' during their trials, thus highlighting the suggested significance and influence of their husbands' coercive behaviour. Both women suggested that it was their husband's control and emotional abuse which led them to be coerced into crime, thus again highlighting the importance of considering the impact of a range of abusive behaviours within the continuum of coercion. Examples of such behaviours are outlined below:

Chris wasn't violent, but he could be very manipulative. If anything was discussed, he would always end up getting his own way. He had a habit of making me feel quite small and inadequate, in fact, I would say to him at times, 'You treat me

like I'm a second year pupil that you used to teach', it was just
the effect he had on me. (Alice Jones, testimony, 17 July 2008)

He was by implication threatening our marriage. I had no choice.
If I didn't return the form, it would be an offence, if I had said
that I had lied, it would mean prosecution for my husband which
would have consequences for the whole family. I had to sign to
preserve our marriage. He would have blamed me forever and
I didn't want another failed marriage behind me. I felt pushed
into a corner and incredibly worn down by his constant pressure
and control. The person that people see in the public eye and
in the press is not the same person that I saw at home.' (Janet
Young, testimony, 26 February 2013)

However, it was questioned by both journalists and legal professionals
(with the exception of their defence teams) how two intelligent,
privileged women could be coerced into crime by their male partner,
yet, by implying that only certain 'types' of women are able to be
coerced, there was a failure to adequately understand the nature of
abusive relationships (Weitzman, 2000). Despite Alice and Janet being
intelligent, well-educated and in Janet's case, privileged, women, this
does not mean that they are devoid of the capacity of being controlled,
abused and coerced by a male partner/husband. Understanding their
cases in the context of the 'continuum of coercion' acknowledges
that their experiences of manipulation and control throughout the
duration of their relationships could have been fully considered when
attempting to explain and understand their suggested experiences of
coercion, rather than simply exploring their relationship within the
context of the offending period.

Conclusion

Overall, rather than continuing to silence, minimise or discredit the
experiences of women who have been coerced into crime by a male
partner, this book offers an alternative way of understanding their

experiences, by utilising concepts such as the 'continuum of coercion' and arguing that such women's offending should be understood within the individual, personal and social context in which it occurred. This 'continuum of coercion' framework highlights that a range of behaviours should be considered as being potentially coercive, such as physical, emotional and economic abuse, control and love and also emphasises that the whole relationship should be explored when attempting to understand coercion as a pathway into crime. Furthermore, such coercive behaviours should be understood as being part of the wider continuum of domestic violence to understand how coercion is able to take place in a variety of relationships and contexts, irrespective of race, culture, education, class and age. Collectively, this approach would lead to a more nuanced understanding and appreciation of coerced women's lived experiences.

SIX
COERCED WOMEN AND CRIMINOLOGY: LOOKING TO THE FUTURE

This concluding chapter discusses the contribution to knowledge provided by this book and considers the ways in which a feminist, critical approach to understanding coercion, may lead to a more holistic criminological understanding of some co-offending women's pathways into crime. It will particularly focus on the issues with dichotomising agency and coercion and viewing victims and offenders as a binary concept when considering the experiences of coerced women. The chapter will also provide a number of recommendations for criminology, particularly considering the ways in which a more nuanced appreciation of co-offending women's experiences could be gained.

Criminology is a discipline, which was developed and created by white, middle-class men, who wanted to understand the experiences of male offenders (Smart, 1976). Women's experiences have been increasingly acknowledged and explored within criminology, mostly due to the contribution of feminist criminology (Smart, 1976; Heidensohn, 1996). With this in mind, this book contributes to this body of knowledge by considering the social construction and experiences of co-offending women and prioritising their voices and perspectives. It is argued here that utilising a feminist approach to understanding coerced women's experiences and representation leads to a more authentic and nuanced appreciation of such women's perspectives.

This book particularly encourages consideration of the issues with dichotomising experiences of agency and coercion within the context of some co-offending women's experiences. Although some feminist scholars argue that women who offend should be viewed as autonomous individuals choosing to commit crime as a conscious and deliberate act, other scholars have argued that women who offend have different motivations to commit crime, some of which render them less than fully autonomous, and women may be influenced by issues such as personal circumstance, poverty or a coercive and/or abusive relationship (Carlen, 1988; Ballinger, 2000; Richie, 1996). Maher (1997) suggests that women who offend are typically viewed to be either independent agents or as lacking control in relation to their offending behaviour. However, this dichotomisation of agency is a reductionist approach, and does not apply to all female offending behaviour, particularly female co-offending which is characterised by coercion and/or abuse.

It is important to note that it is not the intention of this book to deny the agency of all women who offend, but rather that coercion should be understood as being a distinct and often gendered pathway into crime. It is argued here that over-endowing women with agency and denying any potential for coercion in certain co-offending partnerships (which are characterised by a personal relationship, violence, control and/or obsession), may potentially obscure such women's lived experiences and consequently silence their voices and perspective. Coercion may be a difficult concept for many feminist thinkers to comprehend, due the recent emphasis and suggestion that women offenders should be recognised as autonomous beings, who are in control of their offending (Morrisey, 2003). However, although it is acknowledged here that this may reflect the reality of many women's experiences who commit crime, other female offenders, particularly those who suggest that they have been coerced, have different pathways into crime, which are often significantly influenced by abusive and controlling relationships with their male partners/co-offenders. Nevertheless, agency and coercion cannot be understood as being in a binary relationship of presence and absence, where the one is present only by virtue of the other's absence (Madhok et al, 2013). Coercion may exist at varying levels in co-offending relationships, as do experiences of agency and 'choice', thus denying the presence of agency in the presence of coercion (and vice versa) does not reflect the reality of many co-offending women. Acknowledging that both agency and coercion can co-exist in such relationships, albeit at differing levels, enables our understanding to move beyond notions such as 'he made me do it' and rather allows an exploration of how personal, social and cultural context and other mitigating factors may affect such women's perceived offending choices and behaviour.

In addition, the concept of 'coercion into crime' implies that many legal explanations for offending decision-making, such as 'rationality' and 'choice', do not accurately account for the experiences of women who have been coerced into crime by a male partner. According to Madhok et al (2013: 157) 'What matters most is not whether something is chosen, but what it is that is chosen and whether it is worthwhile and beneficial, or at least not detrimental, exploitative and destructive.' With this in mind, in the case studies analysed for this research, although each of the women ultimately made a choice to offend and are not devoid of agency, they each argued that their decision to offend and 'choice' was at least to some extent influenced by their relationship with their male partner. This therefore suggests that the concept of 'rational choice' does not accurately account for the experiences of women who claim to have been coerced into crime by a male partner. Legal and traditional definitions of 'choice' and rationality are male-defined concepts and fail to reflect the reality of many female offenders more generally (Ballinger, 2012) and in particular, women who have been coerced in to crime.

Although this book recognises that both women and men ultimately make a choice to engage in a criminal act, it is argued here that this choice is often influenced by social context, individual circumstance and other external factors. Thus 'choice' needs to be situated in its social context (Daly, 1994). As outlined by Daly (1994: 451, cited in Comack and Brickey 2007: 27) 'It is important to acknowledge, however, that choices are never free and open, that the ability to 'choose' will be affected by broader social conditions.' With this in mind, while each of the women made a 'choice' to offend, it is argued that this 'choice' should have been located in its social context and particularly within the context of their potentially coercive relationship with their male partner/co-offender.

In addition, the 'continuum of coercion' outlined in this book highlights the ways in which a range of potentially coercive behaviours, such as physical, economic, emotional and psychological abuse, love and coercive control may influence and have an impact on co-offending women's pathways into crime and offending 'choices'. The case studies in particular highlight the significance of moving beyond an understanding of coercion as solely physical force and recognising that non-physical techniques, such as control and love, can also be potentially coercive behaviours. Legal and media discourse in particular equates coercion with physical force or threat, as evidenced in the (now abolished) defence of marital coercion. The 'continuum of coercion' attempts to move beyond such simplistic understandings of coerced women's experiences and acknowledges that a range of behaviours should be viewed as being potentially coercive.

By considering the possibility of a continuum of coercion, the varying levels of agency and coercion within different co-offending partnerships are acknowledged, thus enabling a more nuanced account of such women's experiences. With this in mind, it is not suggested here that all women who co-offend with men are coerced into crime and it is recognised that many such women make an autonomous choice, with agency, to engage in such offending behaviour. However, it is argued that co-offending women's relationships, which are characterised by an intimate relationship, control, violence and/or abuse, should be viewed as being potentially coercive and recognised as being a possible influencing factor on such women's pathways into crime and their offending behaviour. This highlights the importance of exploring the whole relationship when considering the possibility of coercion, rather than simply exploring the offending behaviour in isolation. Collectively, rather than the concept of a 'continuum of coercion' being viewed as a framework which denies female offenders responsibility or agency, it is rather a way of attempting to gain a more nuanced understanding of specific co-offending partnerships, which are characterised by coercion, abuse, control and/or obsession and love.

Furthermore, the notion of coercion being a pathway into crime highlights that not all female co-offenders define their offending behaviour as a rational decision or choice, but in the same vein, they cannot be readily and easily defined as a 'victim' of crime. As highlighted by Walklate (2007: 25), despite the distinctions between being a 'deserving' and 'non-deserving victim' being concepts that belonged to the nineteenth century, they have become embedded in twenty-first century policy and culture. Walklate (2007) suggests that due to the socially constructed nature of the term 'victim', being identified as a 'victim' is not a straight-forward process. Becoming a victim involves a process of both the individual recognising that they have been victimised and they must also be recognised as a victim within both policy and socially (Walklate, 2007). If we consider such complexities concerning being defined as a victim, then is clear why there has historically been such a profound dichotomisation between being a victim and an offender within criminological thought. Furthermore, if we consider this alongside Carrabine et al's (2004) notion of a 'hierarchy of victimization', with 'deserving' victims, such as sex workers, being at the bottom of the hierarchy and 'undeserving' victims, such as the elderly, being at the top, the difficulty in where the 'coerced' female offender would fit is evident. The 'coerced' female offender cannot be easily placed into the victim category, particularly the 'ideal' victim. When considering the identities and attributes of victims, Christie (1986) argues that the 'ideal victim' is weak in comparison to the offender, blameless and does not know the offender. Victims who fit within these criteria are more likely to be identified as having an unambiguous, undeniable victim status. With this in mind, the coerced female offender is arguably not blameless, as they also participated in an offending act, the offender is known to them (both because they are themselves an 'offender' and they may not recognise their experiences of coercion as criminal behaviour) and there are multiple layers and facets of 'victim' and 'offender' identities within such cases, which contradicts the traditional image of the singular victim/offender binary.

Traditionally, media, the criminal justice system and criminologists have treated victims and offenders as distinct groups, separate from one another. As highlighted in Chapter Four, the social construction and representation of the co-accused women analysed here highlights that simplistic and gendered motifs were used to explain complicated co-offending relationships, which served to firmly represent the women as not only offenders, but in some instances 'monsters' and 'others', leaving no possibility for experiences of coercion. This consequently served to minimise and silence the women's experiences and perspectives. Furthermore, criminologists have tended to explore the victim–offender overlap within particular contexts, such as criminal involvement increasing one's chance of victimisation more generally (Lauritsen et al, 1991) and exploring the similarities between victims and offenders in terms of demographics and behaviours (Schreck et al, 2008). There has been little exploration within criminology of the victim–offender overlap within the context of coercive relationships. The coerced individual is both a victim and an offender within the same context and potentially at the same point in time, highlighting the unique features of this type of victim–offender overlap. With this in mind, coerced co-offenders highlight the issues with separating victims and offenders into distinct categories, thus evidencing the potentially multi-faceted and multi-layered nature of the victim–offender overlap within such relationships.

Finally, it is argued here that criminologists could also utilise the comparative forms of data (case file material and newspaper articles) used in this study for other criminological research endeavours, particularly those using media methods. By using the case file material as a comparative, corroborative source, this research was able to explore the ways in which journalists reported and represented the legal aspects of the cases. In each of the cases analysed, unsurprisingly, the personal, sensational aspects of the cases were more readily reported on, which supports existing research (Nobles and Schiff, 2004; Jewkes, 2015). However, having the comparative tool of the case file material allowed a more in-depth exploration of the specific ways in which the legal process and trial is reported and which aspects are included or excluded in news media material. Such comparative techniques could be utilised in other research endeavours to enable a comparison between legal and media representations of a range of criminological issues, such as particular offences, criminal actors and/or victims.

Overall, this book contributes to the literature which explores the legal and news media representation of female co-offenders and female offending more broadly (Grabe et al, 2006; Jones and Wardle, 2008; Ballinger, 2012; Jewkes, 2015; Birch, 1996; Wykes and Welsh, 2009; Wykes, 1998). However, this research offers a range of novel contributions to the field, including comparing the legal and news media data of the same cases to explore similarities and differences in representation and focus; it explores the ways in which dominant social constructions of female co-offenders serve to represent such women within gendered motifs and narratives, which consequently silences, mutes and distorts their experiences and finally, the concept of a 'continuum of coercion' is also developed, which aims to offer a more sophisticated conceptualisation of coercion as a pathway into crime. To conclude, this book argues that rather than restricting the co-accused women's reasons for offending to existing ideologies and discourses, which serve to silence and mute their experiences, attempting to understand their point of view and perspective would lead to a more nuanced appreciation of their lived experiences.

References

Adler, F. (1975) *Sisters in crime: The rise of the new female criminal*, New York, NY: McGraw Hill.

Ajzenstadt, M. and Shapira, A. (2012) 'The socio-legal construction of otherness under a neo-liberal regime: The case of foreign workers in Israeli criminal courts', *British Journal of Criminology*, 52: 685–704.

Avelardo, V. (2007) *Mexican American girls and gang violence: Beyond risk*, Basingstoke: Palgrave Macmillan.

Ballinger, A. (2000) *Dead woman walking*, Aldershot: Ashgate.

Ballinger, A. (2011) 'Feminist research, state power and executed women: The case of Louie Calvert', in S. Farrall, M. Hough, S. Maruna and R. Sparks (eds) *Escape routes: Contemporary perspectives of life after punishment*, London: Routledge, pp 107–33.

Ballinger, A. (2012) 'A muted voice from the past: The 'silent silencing' of Ruth Ellis', *Social and Legal Studies*, 21: 445–67.

Barlow, C. (2014) 'Coercion into crime: A gendered pathway into criminality', *Howard League ECAN Bulletin*, October 2014.

Barlow, C. (2015a) 'Documents as 'risky' sources of data: A reflection on social and emotional positioning', *International Journal of Social Research Methodology*, 19: 377–84.

Barlow, C. (2015b) 'Silencing the other: Gendered representations of co-accused women offenders', *Howard Journal of Criminal Justice*, 54: 469–88.

Barlow, C. and Lynes, A. (2015) '(The good), the bag and the ugly: The visual construction of female child sex offenders', *Journalism and Mass Communication*, 5, 480–94.

Barnett, B. (2006) 'Medea in the media: Narrative and myth in newspaper coverage of women who kill their children', *Journalism*, 7: 411–32.

Becker, S. and McCorkel, J.A. (2011) 'The gender of criminal opportunity: The impact of male co-offenders on women's crime', *Feminist Criminology*, 6: 79–110.

Belknap, J. (2007) *The invisible woman: Gender, crime and justice*, Belmont, CA: Wadsworth.

Belknap, J. and Holsinger. K (2006) 'The gendered nature of risk factors for delinquency', *Feminist Criminology*, 1: 48–71.

Bem, S.L. (1993) *The lenses of gender: Transforming the debate on sexual inequality*, New Haven, CT: Yale University Press.

Benedict, H. (1992) *How the press covers sex crimes: Virgin or vamp*, Oxford: Oxford University Press.

Berg, K. (2014) 'Cultural factors in the treatment of battered women with privilege: Domestic violence in the lives of white European-American, middle-class, heterosexual women', *Affilia: Journal of Women and Social Work*, 29: 142–52.

Bernard, J. (1981) 'The good provider role: It's rise and fall', *American Psychologist*, 36: 1–12.

Berrington, E. and Honkatukia, P. (2002) 'An evil monster and a poor thing: Female violence in the media', *Journal of Scandinavian Studies in Criminology and Crime Prevention*, 3: 50–72.

Beveridge, W.I.B. (1951) *The art of scientific investigation*, London: William Heinemann.

Birch, H. (1993) 'If looks could kill: Myra Hindley and the iconography of evil', in H. Birch, *Moving targets: Women, murder and representation*, Virago Press: London, pp 32–61.

Boyle, K. (2005) *Media and violence*, London: Sage Publications.

Brown, V.A. (2007) 'Gang member perpetrated domestic violence: A new conversation', *Journal of Race, Religion, Gender and Class*, 11: 395–413.

Burns, R. (2001) *A theory of the trial*, Princeton, NJ: Princeton University Press.

Butler, J. (1990) *Gender trouble: Feminism and the subversion of identity*, London: Routledge.

Carlen, P. (1988) *Women, crime and poverty*, Milton Keynes: Open University Press.

Carline, A. (2005) 'Women who kill their abusive partners: From sameness to gender construction', *Liverpool Law Review*, 26: 13–44.

Carrabine, E., Iganski, P., Lee, M., Plummer, K. and South, N. (2004) *Criminology: A sociological introduction*, London: Routledge.

Carrington, C. (2002) 'Group crime in Canada', *Canadian Review of Criminology*, 44: 277–315.

Carter, C. and Steiner, L. (eds) (2004) *Critical readings: Media and gender*, London: Open University Press.

Cavaglion, G. (2008) 'Bad, mad or sad? Mothers who kill and press coverage in Israel', *Crime, Media, Culture*, 4: 271–78.

Chesney-Lind, M. (1997) *The female offender: Girls, women and crime*, Thousand Oaks, CA: Sage.

Chesney-Lind, M. and Sheldon, R.G. (2004) *Girls, delinquency and juvenile justice* (3rd edn), Belmont, CA: Wadsworth/Thompson Learning.

Chibnall, S. (1977) *Law and order news: An analysis of crime reporting in the British press*, London: Tavistock.

Christie, N. (1986) 'The ideal victim', in E. Fattah (ed) *From crime policy to victim policy*, Basingstoke: Macmillan, pp 17–30.

Cohen, S. (1972) *Folk devils and moral panics*, Oxford: Martin Robinson.

Cole, P. and Harcup, T. (2010) *Newspaper journalism*, London: Sage.

Comack, E. and Brickey, S. (2007) 'Constituting the violence of criminalized women', *Canadian Journal of Criminology and Criminal Justice*, 49: 1–36.

Cook, J.A. and Fonow, M.M. (1990) 'Knowledge and women's interests: Issues of epistemology and methodology in feminist social research', in J. McCarl Neilsen (ed), *Feminist research methods: Exemplary readings in the social sciences*, Boulder, CO: WestView Press, pp 69–93.

Critcher, C. (2003) *Moral panics and the media*, Oxford: Oxford University Press.

Covington, S. (1988) 'The relational theory of women's psychological development: Implications for the criminal justice system', in R.T. Zaplin (ed), *Female offenders: Critical perspectives and effective interventions*, Gaithersburg, MD: Aspen Publishers, pp 113–31.

Daily Mail (2002) 'Loner who found wife in bed with his brother, and the girlfriend with a bee tattoo on her breast', *Daily Mail*, 20 August.

Daily Mail (2003a) 'Misfit who lied for her lover', *Daily Mail*, 18 December.

Daily Mail (2003b) '*Sarah*: Why I believe she is the new Myra', *Daily Mail*, 18 December.

Daily Mail (2003c) '*Sarah Johnson* told police she was in the bath the night *Lucy* and *Katie* dies. This is what she was really doing', *Daily Mail*, 18 December.

Daily Mail (2003d) 'I picked Jessica up, took her downstairs and went back for Holly: I put the bodies in my car and drove', *Daily Mail*, 2 December.

Daily Mail (2007) 'The canoe caper is a perfect farce of our times', *Daily Mail*, 12 December.

Daily Mail (2009a) 'Facebook strangers bound by depravity', *Daily Mail*, 2 October.

Daily Mail (2009b) 'Agony for hundreds of families at abuse nursery', *Daily Mail*, 2 October.

Daily Mail (2009c) 'I'll never call her mum again, says daughter of nursery paedophile', *Daily Mail*, 5 October.

Daily Mail (2009d) 'From a bubbly, happy mother to "your paedo whore mumma"', *Daily Mail*, 16 December.

Daily Mail (2009e) 'Parents' fury over nursery nurse who called herself "paedo whore mumma"', *Daily Mail*, 16 December.

Daily Mail (2010) 'The depravity that made nursery "ideal" for abuse', *Daily Mail*, 5 November.

Daily Mail (2013) 'The *price* of vengeance', *Daily Mail*, 8 March.

Daily Star (2002) 'Driven wild by her lust', *Daily Star*, 19 August.

REFERENCES

Daily Star (2003) '*Sarah* noisy sex upset neighbours', *Daily Star*, 18 December.

Daily Star (2007) 'We're sunk: Cheating canoe plot wife says', *Daily Star*, 6 December.

Daily Star (2009a) 'Height of depravity', *Daily Star*, 2 October.

Daily Star (2009b) 'Perv arrest mum is a nursery worker: New torment for parents', *Daily Star*, 14 October.

Daily Telegraph (2002) 'Rootless and troubled lives of couple suspected of killing *Lucy* and *Katie*', *Daily Telegraph*, 20 August.

Daily Telegraph (2007a) 'A merry widow or a grieving one? A fake passport for her 'dead' husband, two devastated sons and money in the bank', *Daily Telegraph*, 8 December.

Daily Telegraph (2007b) 'They were planning eco-centre for kayak fans', *Daily Telegraph*, 8 December.

Daily Telegraph (2009) 'The abusers: 'Devilish' alliance formed after chance meeting on Facebook', *Daily Telegraph*, 2 October.

Daly, K. (1994) *Gender, crime and punishment*, New Haven, CT: Yale University Press.

Daly, K. and Chesney-Lind, M. (1988) 'Feminism and criminology', in P. Cordella and L. Siegel (eds) *Readings in contemporary criminological theory*, Boston, MA: Northeastern University Press, pp 340–64.

Davidson, J.C. (2008) 'Child sexual abuse: Media representations and government reactions', *Internet Journal of Criminology*, ISSN 2045–6743.

Davies, M. (1997) 'Taking the inside out: Sex and gender in the legal subject', in N. Naffine and R.J. Owens (eds) *Sexing the subject of law*, London: Sweet and Maxwell, pp 25–46.

Denov, M. (2004) *Perspectives on female sex offending: A culture of denial*, Aldershot: Ashgate Publishing.

Dombrowski, S.C., Gischlar, K.L. and Durst, T. (2007) 'Safeguarding young people from cyber pornography and cyber sexual predation: A major dilemma of the internet', *Child Abuse Review*, 16: 153–70.

Eckstein, J.J. (2011) 'Reasons for staying in intimately violent relationships: Comparisons of men and women and messages communicated to self and others', *Journal of Family Violence*, 26: 21–30.

Edwards, S.M. (1984) *Women on trial: A study of the female suspect, defendant and offender in the criminal law and Criminal Justice System*, Manchester: Manchester University Press.

Ellis, H. (1984) *Man and woman: A study of human secondary characteristics*, London: Walter Scott.

England, K. (1994) 'Getting personal: Reflexivity, positionality and feminist research', *The Professional Geographer*, 46: 241–56.

Entman, R. (1993) 'Framing: Toward clarification of a fractured paradigm', *Journal of Communication*, 43: 51–8.

Ericson, R.V., Baranek, P.M. and Chan, J.B.L. (1991) *Representing order: Crime, law and justice in news media*, Milton Keynes: Open University Press.

Evans, K. and Jamieson, J. (2008) *Gender and crime: A reader*, Berkshire: Open University Press.

Express (2003a) 'The real story', *Express*, 18 December.

Express (2003b) 'World exclusive picture: *Johnson* snogging a teenager on the very night that *Lucy* and *Katie* died; sex-mad *Sarah*', *Express*, 18 December.

Express (2009) 'The twisted trio of perverts', *Express*, 2 October.

Express (2013) '*Young* brought down by her hunger for vengeance', *Express*, 8 March.

Feilezer, M.Y. (2007) 'Criminologists making news? Providing factual information about crime and criminal justice through a weekly newspaper column', *Crime, Media, Culture*, 3: 285–304.

Ferrell, J., Hayward, K., Morrison, W. and Presdee, M. (2004) *Cultural criminology unleashed*, London: Glasshouse Press.

Flyvbjerg, B. (2006) 'Five misunderstandings about case study research, *Qualitative Inquiry*', 12: 219–45.

Franklin, B. (2003) 'A good day to buy bad news? Journalists, sources and the packaging of politics', in S. Cottle (ed) *News, public relations and power*, London: Sage.

Friedan, B. (1963) *The feminist mystique*, London: Penguin.

French, S. (1996) 'Partners in crime', in A. Myers and S. Wight (eds) *No angels: Women who commit violence*, London: Pandora.

Gavin, H. (2009) '"Mummy wouldn't do that": The perception and construction of the female child sex abuser', *Evil, women and the feminine*, 1–3 May, Budapest, Hungary.

Gelsthorpe, L. (2003) *Exercising discretion: Decision making in the criminal justice system and beyond*, London: Willan.

Gilligan, C. (1982) *In a different voice: Psychological theory and women's development*, Cambridge, MA: Harvard University Press.

Grabe, M., Trager, K.D., Lear, M. and Rauch, J. (2006) 'Gender in crime news: A case study test of the chivalry hypothesis', *Mass Communication and Society*, 9: 137–63.

Graber, D. (1980) *Crime news and the public*, New York, NY: Praeger.

Greer, C. (2003) 'Sex crime and the media: Press representations in Northern Ireland', in P. Mason (ed) *Criminal visions*, Cullompton: Willan.

Guardian (2003) 'I've been feeling very, very guilty for a long time', *Guardian*, 5 December.

Guardian (2007) 'In custody: The canoeist snapped smiling despite being declared dead', *Guardian*, 6 December.

Guardian (2008) '*Simon Jones* canoe disappearance: A modern mystery: Canoe couple *Simon* and *Alice Jones*', *Guardian*, 25 July.

Guardian (2009) 'Nursery paedophile case: The offenders: Connected online, abusers never met', *Guardian*, 2 October.

Guardian (2013) '*Janet Young* trial: Vengeance, a pyrrhic victory – and now two careers are left in tatters', *Guardian*, 8 March.

Harding, S. (1981) *Feminism and methodology: Social science issues*, Bloomington, IN: Indiana University Press.

Harding, S. (1991) *Whose science? Whose knowledge? Thinking from women's lives*, Ithaca, NY: Cornell University Press.

Hayes, S. and Baker, B. (2014) 'Female sex offenders and pariah femininities: Rewriting the sexual scripts', *Journal of Criminology*, dx.doi.org/10.1155/2014/414525.

Hebenton, B. and Seddon, T. (2009) 'From dangerousness to precaution: Managing sexual and violent offenders in an insecure and uncertain age', *British Journal of Criminology*, 49: 343–62.

Heidensohn, F. (1996) *Women and crime* (2nd edn), Basingstoke: Macmillan.

Heidensohn, F. (2002) 'Gender and crime,' in M. Maguire, R. Morgan and R. Reiner (eds), *The Oxford handbook of criminology*, Oxford: Oxford University Press, pp 491–530.

Henry-Waring, M. and Barraket, J. (2008) 'Dating and intimacy in the 21st century: The use of online dating sites in Australia', *International Journal of Emerging Technologies and Society*, 6: 14–33.

Herriott, R.E. and Firestone, W.A. (1983) 'Multisite qualitative policy research: Optimising description and generalisability', *Educational Researcher*, 12: 14–19.

HMCTS Case File (2002–03) *Sarah Johnson case file* (Unpublished legal documents). Held at Old Bailey Crown Court.

HMCTS Case File (2007–08) *Anne Darwin case file* (Unpublished legal documents). Held at Teesside Crown Court.

HMCTS Case File (2009–10) *Jane Turner case file* (Unpublished legal documents). Held at Bristol Crown Court.

HMCTS Case File (2012–13) *Janet Young case file* (Unpublished legal documents). Held at Southwark Crown Court.

Independent (2003a) '*Johnson* turns on "abusive and controlling", Fox', *Independent*, 5 December.

Independent (2003b) 'A dreadful journey from innocence to horror and, eventually, to justice', *Independent*, 18 December.

Independent on Sunday (2007) 'Police charge *Jones* with fraud', *Independent on Sunday*, 9 December.

Inglis, T. (2003) *Truth, power and lies*, Dublin: University College Dublin Press.

Jacques, H.A.K. and Radtke, H.L. (2012) 'Constrained by choice: Young women negotiate the discourse of marriage and motherhood', *Feminism and Psychology*, 22: 443–61.

Jewkes, Y. (2015) *Media and crime*, London: Sage

Jones, P. and Wardle, C. (2008) '"No emotion, no sympathy": The visual construction of Maxine Carr', *Crime, Media and Culture*, 4: 53–71.

Jones, P. and Wardle, C. (2010) 'Hindley's ghost: the visual construction of Maxine Carr', in K. Hayward and M. Presdee (eds) *Framing crime: Cultural criminology and the image*, London: Routledge.

Jones, S. (2008) 'Partners in crime: A study of the relationship between female offenders and their co-defendants', *Criminology and Criminal Justice*, 8: 147–64.

Jones, S. (2011) 'Under pressure: Women who plead guilty to crimes they have not committed', *Criminology and Criminal Justice*, 11: 77–90.

Katz, R. (2000) 'Explaining girls' and women's crime and desistance in the context of their victimization experiences', *Violence Against Women*, 6(6): 633–60.

Kelly, L. (1988) *Surviving sexual violence*, Cambridge: Polity.

Kennedy, M., Klein, C., Bristowe, J., Cooper, B. and Yuille, J. (2007) 'Routes of recruitment: Pimps' techniques and other circumstances that lead to street prostitution', *Journal of Aggression, Maltreatment and Trauma*, 15: 1–19.

Kincaid, J.R. (1998) *Erotic innocence: The culture of child molesting*, London: Duke University Press.

Kirsta, A. (1994) *Deadlier than the male*, London: HarperCollins.

Kitzinger, J. (2004) *Framing abuse: Media influence and public understanding of sexual violence against children*, London: Pluto.

Koons-Witt, B. and Schram, P.J. (2003) 'The prevalence and nature of violent offending by females', *Journal of Criminal Justice*, 31: 361–71.

Lauritsen, J.L., Sampson, R.J. and Laub, J.H. (1991) 'The link between offending and victimization among adolescents', *Criminology*, 29: 265–92.

Lavie-Dinur, A., Karniel, Y. and Azran, T. (2013) '"Bad girls": The use of gendered media frames in the Israeli media's coverage of Israeli female political criminals', *Journal of Gender Studies*, 22: 1–21.

Letherby, G. (2003) *Feminist research in theory and practice*, Buckingham: Open University Press.

Lloyd, A. (1995) *Doubly deviant, doubly damned: Society's treatment of violent women*, Penguin: London.

Lombroso, C. and Ferrero, W. (1895) *The female offender*, London: Fisher Unwin.

McGloin, J.M., Sullivan, C.J., Piquero, A. and Bacon, S. (2008) 'Investigating the stability of co-offending and co-offenders among a sample of youthful offenders', *Criminology*, 46: 155–88.

Machado, H. and Santos, F. (2009) 'The disappearance of Madeline McCann: Public drama and trial by the media in Portuguese press', *Crime and Media Culture*, 5: 146–67.

Madhok, S., Phillips, A. and Wilson, K. (2013) *Gender, agency and coercion*, Palgrave: London.

Mail on Sunday (2013) 'Every couple should take some points from the howling *Crouches*, *Mail on Sunday*, 10 February.

Maher, L. (1997) *Sexed work: Gender, race and resistance in a Brooklyn drug market*, Oxford: Clarendon Press.

Matthews, J.K., Matthews, R. and Speltz, K. (1991) 'Female sex offenders: A typology', in M.Q. Patton (ed), *Family sexual abuse: Frontline research and evaluation*, Newsbury Park, CA: Sage, pp 199–219.

Mirror (2007a) 'What have I done? Exclusive mysterious Mr Canoe's mum's grief as boys disown her', *Mirror*, 7 December.

Mirror (2007b) 'I'm feeling sick to my stomach. Exclusive: Canoe wife arrested. *Alice's* tears and panic as armed cops board plane', *Mirror*, 10 December.

Mirror (2008a) 'Their eyes did not meet: There's no forgiveness. Canoe couple guilty: Betrayed sons disown parents', *Mirror*, 24 July.

Mirror (2008b) 'Losing her sons is the worst sentence for *Alice Jones*', *Mirror*, 26 July.

Mirror (2009a) 'Police: Tell us who you took pictures of… As a mum you'd want to know. Don't you care? *Turner*: No comment; Nursery paedo's sickening police tapes', *Mirror*, 13 October.

Mirror (2009b) '5th person in paedo ring is convicted', *Mirror*, 19 October.

Mirror (2009c) 'Nursery paedo to get new identity: Death threats to evil mum', *Mirror*, 16 December.

Mirror (2009d) 'A new depth of depravity: Judge blasts vile mum *Turner* as she is jailed', *Mirror*, 16 December.

Mirror (2013) 'So was is really worth it, *Janet?*', *Mirror*, 10 March.

Morrisey, B. (2003) *When women kill: Questions of agency and subjectivity*, London: Routledge.

Mosselson, J. (2010) 'Subjectivity and reflexivity: Locating the self in research on dislocation', *International Journal of Qualitative Studies in Education*, 23: 479–94.

Mullins, C. and Wright, R. (2003) 'Gender social networks and residential burglary', *Criminology*, 41: 813–40.

Murphy, T. and Whitty, N. (2006) The question of evil and feminist legal scholarship, *Feminist Legal Studies*, 14: 1–26.

Myers, A. and Wight, S. (1996) *No angels: Women who commit violence*, London: Pandora.

Naffine, N. (1987) *Female crime: The construction of women in criminology*, London: Allen Unwin.

Naffine, N. (1996) *Feminism and criminology*, Philadelphia, PA: Temple University Press.

Naylor, B. (2001) 'Reporting violence in the British print media: Gendered stories', *The Howard Journal*, 40: 180–94.

Nobles, R. and Schiff, D. (2004) 'A story of miscarriage of justice: Law in the media', *Journal of Law and Society*, 31: 221–4.

Oakley, A. (1992) *Social support and motherhood: the natural history of a research project*, Oxford: Blackwell.

People (2002) 'Weird sex, scratching, biting and stilettoes…our hell in bizarre world of *Sarah*: Ex-lovers reveal the disturbing night-time secrets of accused girlfriend', *People*, 25 August.

People (2003) '*Sarah* is a pervert; *Lucy* and *Katie* monster: Shocking revelations', *People*, 21 December.

People (2007) 'Ultimate betrayal that left them all in pieces: Mr and Mrs Canoe saga tears family apart', *People*, 9 December.

People (2009) 'Monster at work: Nursery paedo pic EXCLUSIVE', *People*, 4 October.

Pettersson, T (2005) 'Gendering delinquent networks: A gendered analysis of violent crimes and the structure of boys and girls co-offending networks', *Young Nordic Journal of Youth Research*, 13: 247–67.

Pollack, O. (1950/1961) *The criminality of women*, New York, NY: AS, Barnes/Perpetua.

Reiss, A.J., Jr. and Farrington, D.P. (1991) 'Advancing knowledge about co-offending: Results from a prospective longitudinal survey of London males', *Journal of Criminal Law and Criminology*, 82: 360–95.

Richie, B.E. (1996) *Compelled to crime: The gender entrapment of battered black women*, New York, NY: Routledge.

Riggins, S.H. (1997) *The language and politics of exclusion*, Thousand Oaks, CA: Sage.

Ross, K. (2007) 'The journalist, the housewife, the citizen and the press: Women and men in local news narratives', *Journalism*, 8: 449–73.

Russett, C.E. (1989) *Sexual science: The Victorian construction of womanhood*, London: Harvard University Press.

Sanders, T., O'Neill, M. and Pitcher, J. (2009) *Prostitution: Sex work, policy and politics*, London: Sage.

Schreck, C.J., Stewart, E.A. and Osgood, D.W. (2008) 'A reappraisal of the overlap of violent offenders and victims', *Criminology*, 46, 871–906.

Simpson, J. and Speake, J. (2009) 'Hell hath no fury like a woman scorned', *Oxford Dictionary of Proverbs*, www.oxfordreference.com/view/10.1093/acref/9780199539536.001.0001/acref-9780199539536-e-1046.

Skilbrei, M.L. (2013) 'Sisters in crime: Representations of gender and class in the media coverage and court proceedings of the triple homicide at Orderud Farm', *Crime, Media, Culture*, 9: 136–52.

Smart, C. (1976) *Women, crime and criminology*, London: Routledge.

Smart, C. (1989) *Feminism and the power of the law*, London: Routledge.

Soothill, K. and Walby, S. (1991) *Sex crime in the news*, London: Routledge.

Stanley, L. and Wise, S. (1993) *Breaking out again: Feminist ontology and epistemology*, London: Routledge.

Stark, E. (2007) *Coercive control: How men entrap women in personal life*, London: Oxford University Press.

Steedman, C. (2001) *Dust*, Manchester: Manchester University Press.

Steedman, C. (2013) 'Archival methods', in G. Griffin (ed), *Research methods for English students*, Edinburgh: Edinburgh University Press.

Sun (2003) 'Kiss of death', *Sun*, 18 December.

Sun (2009a) 'Nursery parents wept as they left meeting with cops', *Sun*, 11 June.

Sun (2009b) 'How could a MOTHER abuse these kids?', *Sun*, 3 October.

Sun (2009c) 'Nursery paedo whore is caged', *Sun*, 16 December.

Sun (2009d) 'Nursery paedo's "let off"; Just 7 yrs', *The Sun*, 16 December.

Sun (2013a) 'I want to nail him; Ex wife's fury over *Crouch* affair', *Sun*, 6 February.

Sun (2013b) '*Crouch* kids paying *price* for vile pair', *Sun*, 9 March.

Sunday Telegraph (2007) 'How the Simon and Alice Jones story evolved', *Sunday Telegraph*, 9 December.

Sunday Times (2013) '"I cared for him a lot. I was very much in love": The trial of *Janet Young* has provided a searing insight into the implosion of her marriage to *Edward Crouch*', *Sunday Times*, 10 February.

Surette, R. (1998) *Media, crime, and criminal justice: Images and realities*, Belmont, CA: Wadworth.

Syed, F. and Williams, S. (1996) *Case studies of female sex offenders in the Correctional Service of Canada*, Ottawa: Correctional Service Canada.

Sydie, R.A. (1987) *Natural women, cultured men: A feminist perspective on Sociological theory*, Milton Keynes: Open University Press.

Tankard, J.W. (2001) 'The empirical approach to the study of media framing', in S.D. Reese, O.H. Gandy and A.E. Grant (eds) *Framing public life*, Mahwah, NJ: Lawrence Erlbaum, pp 95–106.

The Times (2002) 'Couple charged over girls' murder', *The Times*, 21 August.

The Times (2003) 'I'm not going to be blamed for what that thing in that box has done', *The Times*, 5 December.

The Times (2007) 'The wrath of the sons is visited upon the father – and mother', *The Times*, 7 December.

The Times (2008) 'Duped sons were the real victims, judge tells court', *The Times*, 24 July.

The Times (2009a) 'Women abused toddlers in their care for Facebook "friend" they had never met', *The Times*, 2 October.

The Times (2009b) 'Paedophile nursery worker may never be released; Judge demands that she names her victims', *The Times*, 16 December.

The Times (2013a) 'I want to nail him: *Crouch* wife "plotted her revenge"', *The Times*, 6 February.

The Times (2013b) 'Jury asked to decide if *Janet Young* is weak-minded or manipulative woman', *The Times*, 6 February.

The Times (2013c) 'Legal relic of the Middle Ages', *The Times*, 8 March.

Thomas, G. (2010) 'Doing case study. Abduction not induction: Phronesis not theory', *Qualitative Inquiry*, 16: 575–81.

Walklate, S. (2001) *Gender crime and criminal justice*, Uffculme: Willan Publishing.

Walklate, S. (2007) *Imagining the victim of crime*, Berkshire: Open University Press.

Warr, M. (1996) 'Organization and instigation in delinquent groups', *Criminology*, 36: 11–37.

Weitzman, S. (2000) *Not to people like us: Hidden abuse in upscale marriages*, New York: Basic Books.

Welle, D. and Falkin, G. (2000) 'The everyday policing of women with romantic co-defendants: An ethnographic perspective', *Women and Criminal Justice*, 11: 45–65.

West, C. and Zimmerman, D.H. (1987) 'Doing gender', *Gender and Society*, 125, 125–51.

Wood, J.T. (2001) 'The normalization of violence in heterosexual romantic relationships: Women's narratives of love and violence', *Journal of Social and Personal Relationships*, 18: 239–61.

Wykes, M. (1998) 'A family affair: The British press, sex and the Wests', in C. Carter, G. Branston and S. Allen (eds) *News, gender and power*, London: Routledge.

Wykes, M. and Gunter, B. (2005) *The media and body image: If looks could kill*, London: Sage.

Wykes, M. and Welsh, K. (2009) *Violence, gender and Justice*, London: Sage.

Villani, S.L. and Ryan, J. (1997) *Motherhood at the crossroads: Meeting the challenge of a changing role*, New York, NY: Insight Books.

Yeo, S. (1993) 'Resolving gender bias in criminal defences', *Monash University Law Review*, 19: 104–16.

Yin, R.K. (2009) *Case study research: Design and methods*, London: Sage.

Young, J. (1999) *The exclusive society*, London: Sage.

Index

Printed and bound by CPI Group (UK) Ltd, Croydon, CR0 4YY

13/04/2025

14656588-0002